AF380672

NCERT EXEMPLAR

Problems-Solutions

Science

Detailed Explanation to all Objective
& Subjective Problems

6

Kriti Sharma • Seema Mehra • Sikha Sharma

ARIHANT
PRAKASHAN, MEERUT

All rights reserved

卐 © Publisher
No part of this publication may be re-produced, stored in a retrieval system or distributed in any form or by any means, electronic, mechanical, photocopying, recording, scanning, web or otherwise without the written permission of the publisher. Arihant has obtained all the information in this book from the sources believed to be reliable and true. However, Arihant or its editors or authors or illustrators dont take any responsibility for the absolute accuracy of any information published, and the damages or loss suffered thereupon.

卐 Administrative & Production Offices
Corporate Office: 'Ramchhaya' 4577/15, Agarwal Road, Darya Ganj, New Delhi -110002
Tele: 011- 47630600, 43518550; Fax: 011- 23280316

Head Office: Kalindi, TP Nagar, Meerut (UP) - 250002
Tele: 0121-2401479, 2512970, 4004199; Fax: 0121-2401648

All disputes subject to Meerut (UP) jurisdiction only.

卐 Sales & Support Offices
Agra, Ahmedabad, Bengaluru, Bhubaneswar, Bareilly, Chennai, Delhi, Guwahati, Haldwani Hyderabad, Jaipur, Jalandhar, Jhansi, Kolkata, Kota, Lucknow, Meerut, Nagpur & Pune

卐 ISBN 978-93-5251-149-5

卐 Price : ₹ 75

PRINTED & BOUND BY
ARIHANT PUBLICATIONS (I) LTD. (PRESS UNIT)

For further information about the products from Arihant
log on to www.arihantbooks.com or email to info@arihantbooks.com

PREFACE

The Department of Education in Science & Mathematics (DESM) & National Council of Educational Research & Training (NCERT) developed Exemplar Problems in Science and Mathematics for Upper Primary Stage, Secondary and Senior Secondary Classes with the objective to provide the students a large number of quality problems in various forms and format viz. Multiple Choice Questions, Short Answer Questions, Long Answer Questions etc., with varying levels of difficulty.

The problems given in Exemplar books are not meant to some merely as question bank for examination but are Primarily meant to improve the quality of teaching/ learning process in schools and finally will impart the problem solving skills in students and it is a widely at acknowledged fact that in this century analytical thinking, problem solving ability, creativity and speculative ability will be key skills for success.

This book **NCERT Exemplar Problems-Solutions Science VI** contains Explanatory & Accurate Solutions to all the questions given in NCERT Exemplar Science book.

For the overall benefit of the students we have made unique this book in such a way that it presents not only hints and solutions but also detailed and authentic explanations. Through these detailed explanations, students can learn the concepts which will enhance their thinking and learning abilities.

For the completion of this book, we would like to thank Mr. Prince Mittal (Project Coordinator, Arihant Prakashan) who helped us at project management level.

With the hope that this book will be of great help to the students, we wish great success to our readers.

Authors

CONTENTS

1. Food : Where Does It Come From? — 1-6
2. Components of Food — 7-15
3. Fibre to Fabric — 16-21
4. Sorting Materials and Groups — 22-28
5. Separation of Substances — 29-35
6. Changes Around Us — 36-40
7. Getting to Know Plants — 41-47
8. Body Movement — 48-52
9. The living Organisms and Their Surroundings — 53-59
10. Motion and Measurement of Distances — 60-68
11. Light — 69-75
12. Electricity and Circuits — 76-82
13. Fun with Magnets — 83-89
14. Water — 90-93
15. Air Around Us — 94-99
16. Garbage In, Garbage Out — 100-107

1

Food : Where Does It Come From?

Multiple Choice Questions (MCQs)

Q. 1 Given below are the names of some animals.

    (i) Goat   (ii) Human beings

    (iii) Cockroach   (iv) Eagle

Which of the above animals form a pair of omnivores?

    (a) (i) and (ii)   (b) (ii) and (iii)

    (c) (iii) and (iv)   (d) (ii) and (iv)

Ans. *(b)* Animals that eat both plants and animals are called **Omnivores**.

e.g. Human beings, cockroach, wood peckers, etc.

Herbivores are plant eaters, e.g. Goat, sheep, horse, etc.

Carnivores are meat eaters, e.g. Eagle, cheetah, etc.

Q. 2 Honeybee makes honey from

    (a) pollen   (b) petals   (c) nectar   (d) bud

Ans. *(c)* A honeybee starts the honey making process by visiting flower(s) and gathering some of its nectar (sweet juices).

This nectar is converted into honey and stored in their hives.

Q. 3 Below are the names of some animals.

    (i) Cow   (ii) Sheep

    (iii) Horse   (iv) Ox

Which of the above are the sources of milk for human beings?

    (a) (i) and (iii)   (b) (i) and (ii)

    (c) (ii) and (iii)   (d) (iii) and (iv)

Ans. *(b)* Cow and sheep are the sources of milk for human beings.

Q. 4 Given below is a list of edible plants.

(i) Banana   (ii) Pumpkin

(iii) Lady's finger   (iv) Brinjal

Which pair of plants has two or more edible parts?

(a) (i) and (ii)   (b) (ii) and (iii)

(c) (iii) and (iv)   (d) (i) and (iv)

Ans. *(a)* Banana and pumpkin plant has two or more edible parts. Their flowers and fruits are eaten as food. Brinjal and lady's finger only have their fruit as the edible part.

Q. 5 The part of a banana plant not used as food is

(a) flower   (b) fruit

(c) stem   (d) root

Ans. *(d)* All parts of banana (i.e. fruit, leaves, flowers and stems) except roots are edible.

Q. 6 Read each set of terms and identify the odd set.

(a) Cow, milk, butter

(b) Hen, meat, egg

(c) Goat, milk, meat

(d) Plant, vegetable, butter, milk

Ans. *(d)* In each set, the term with its edible sources are given.

(d) is the odd set because butter and milk are not obtained from plant.

Very Short Answer Type Questions

Q. 7 Read the clues and fill up the blanks given below each of them.

(a) Honeybees suck this from flower. N _ _ T _ R

(b) Animals which eat other animals. _ A _ N _ V _ R _ S

(c) Animals which eat only plants and plant products. H E _ B _ _ _ _ _ E _

(d) Animals which eat both plants and animals. _ M N I _ O _ _ _

Ans. (a) NECTAR   (b) CARNIVORES

(c) HERBIVORES   (d) OMNIVORES

Q. 8 Why do boiled seeds fail to sprout?

Ans. The boiled seeds failed to sprout because boiling denatures or damages certain enzymes or proteins that are required for germination. Thus, boiling kills the seeds.

Q. 9 Where do bees store honey?

Ans. The bees store honey in their nest which is known as beehive. It is a densely packed group of hexagonal cells made of beeswax (honeycomb).

Q. 10 Name two ingredients in our food that are not obtained from plants or animals. Mention one source for each ingredient.

Ans. The two ingredients in our food that are not obtained from plants or animals are:

    (i) **Salt** It is obtained from seawater and rocks.

    (ii) **Water** It is obtained from river/tap/pond/lake/rain.

Q. 11 Given below are jumbled words, which are names of parts of a plant. Rearrange them to get the correct words.

    (a) LILCHI   (b) ITRUF

    (c) SEANBOYA   (d) GURSA

    (e) ROUNDGUNT

Ans. (a) CHILLI   (b) FRUIT

    (c) SOYABEAN   (d) SUGAR

    (e) GROUNDNUT

Short Answer Type Questions

Q. 12 Identify the animals in the grid given below and categorise them into herbivore, carnivore and omnivore.

T	A	C	O	W	O	L	F
T	A	R	W	X	G	O	R
N	N	O	L	I	O	N	O
E	T	W	Q	L	A	N	G
H	U	M	A	N	T	W	O

Ans.

T	A	C	O	W	O	L	F
T	A	R	W	X	G	O	R
N	N	O	L	I	O	N	O
E	T	W	Q	L	A	N	G
H	U	M	A	N	T	W	O

These can be categorised as :

Herbivore (plant eating animals) COW, GOAT, HEN

Carnivore (meat eating animals) WOLF, LION, FROG

Omnivore (eats both plants and meat) HUMAN, RAT, CAT, CROW, OWL, ANT

Q. 13 Why should we avoid wastage of food?

Ans. We should avoid wastage of food because

   (i) There are many people amongst us, who do not get sufficient food, due to the lack of money.

   (ii) Enough food is not available for all of us.

Q. 14 Why do organisms need food? Write two reasons.

Ans. Food is needed by organisms for the following reasons:

   (i) Food provides us energy to perform various functions of life.

   (ii) Food helps to protect the body against various diseases and infections.

Q. 15 Match the organisms given in column I with their part/product in column II that is used by human beings as food.

	Column I		Column II
(a)	Mustard plant	(i)	Meat
(b)	Goat	(ii)	Fruits and vegetable
(c)	Hen	(iii)	Seed
(d)	Smoke	(iv)	Direction of air flow
(e)	Wind	(v)	Prevent dust particles

Ans. The correct matching is:

(a)—(iii),   (b)—(i),   (c)—(iv),   (d)—(v),   (e)—(ii)

(a) Seeds of mustard plant are used to extract oils.

(b) Goat's meat is called chevon or mutton.

(c) A windvane or weather cock is an instrument for showing the direction of the wind. It has a hen (cockerel design) on the top.

(d) Smoke and dust are two major components of particulate matter that should be prevented.

(e) Wind has both direct and indirect effects on plant growth, fruits and vegetable.

Q. 16 Label the different parts of the plant given below in figure.

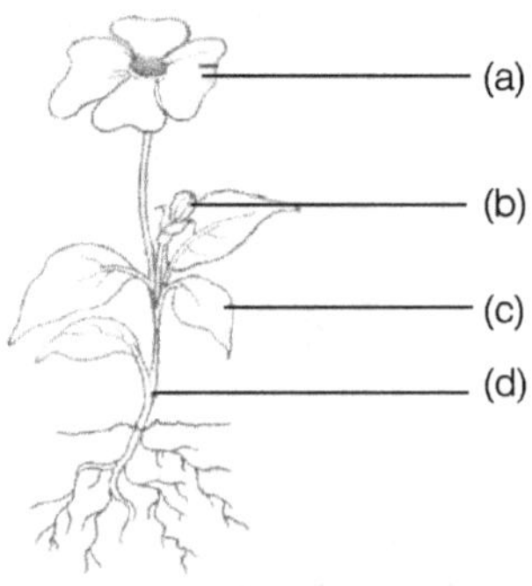

Ans. The different parts of the plant as labelled correctly are:

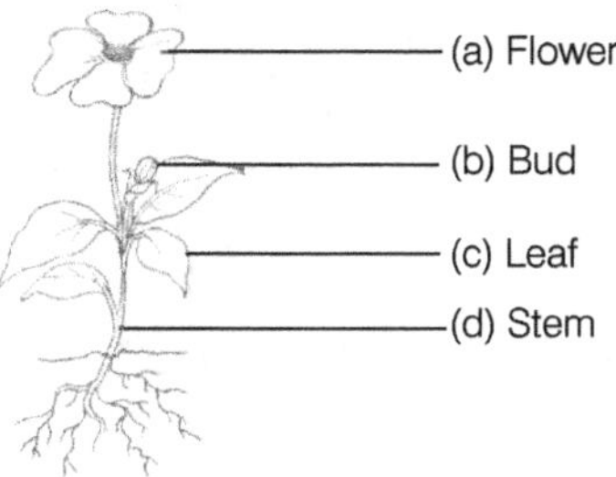

Long Answer Type Questions

Q. 17 Read the names of animals written in the inner ring of the figure. Within the second ring, write the types of food they eat and the category to which they belong (based on the eating habit) in the outermost ring. One example has been worked out for you.

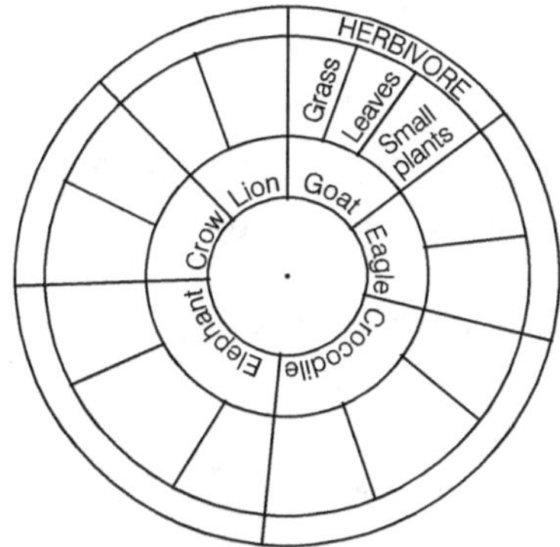

Ans. The completely filled ring is as given below:

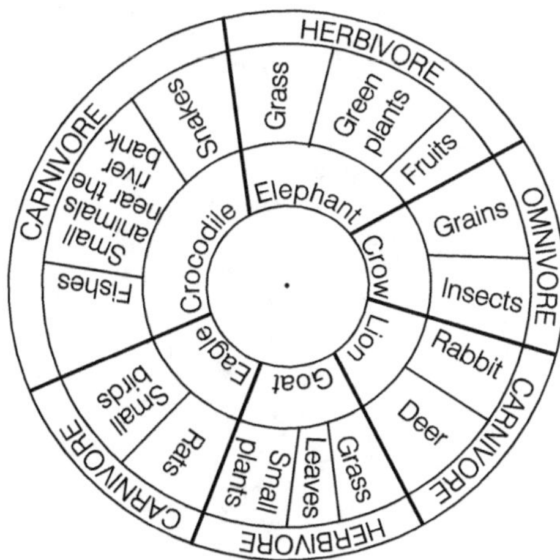

Q. 18 Connect the animal with the food it eats by an arrow using different colours in the figure given below. One is done for you.

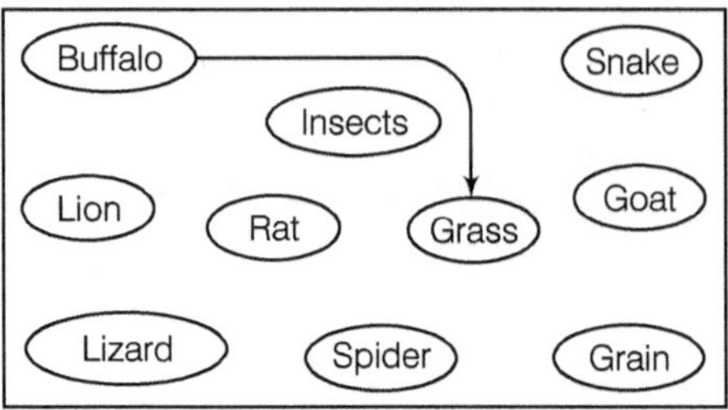

Ans. The complete figure is as follows:

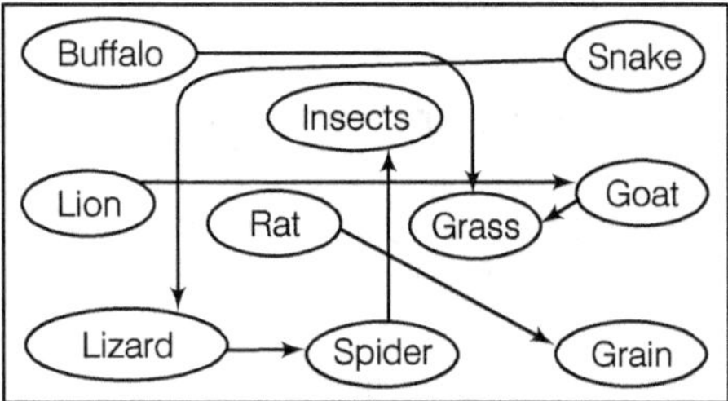

Q. 19 List two of your favourite food items and mention their ingredients.

Ans. The two favourite food items and their ingredients are:

Food items	Ingredients
Kheer	Rice, milk and sugar
Idli	Rice, urad dal, salt and water

2

Components of Food

Multiple Choice Questions (MCQs)

Q. 1 Which one of the following food items does not provide dietary fibre?

    (a) Whole grains   (b) Whole pulses

    (c) Fruits and vegetables   (d) Milk

Ans. *(d)* Milk does not provide dietary fibre. It is an excellent source of vitamins, proteins and minerals particularly calcium.

The other three, i.e. whole grains, whole pulses, fresh fruits and vegetables are main source of roughage or dietary fibres. Roughage helps our body to get rid of undigested food.

Q. 2 Which of the following sources of protein is different from others?

    (a) Peas   (b) Grams

    (c) Soyabeans   (d) Cottage cheese (paneer)

Ans. *(d)* Among the given sources of protein, cottage cheese (paneer) is different as it is an animal protein, whereas peas, grams and soyabeans are plant proteins.

Q. 3 Which of the following nutrients is not present in milk?

    (a) Protein   (b) Vitamin-C   (d) Calcium   (d) Vitamin-D

Ans. *(b)* Vitamin-C is not present in milk. It is present in citrus fruits, such as oranges and green vegetables.

Q. 4 Read the food items given below.

    (i) Wheat   (ii) Ghee

    (iii) Iodised salt   (iv) Spinach (palak)

Which of the above food items are energy giving foods?

    (a) (i) and (iv)   (b) (ii) and (iv)   (c) (i) and (ii)   (d) (iii) and (iv)

Ans. *(c)* Wheat (i.e. carbohydrates) and Ghee (i.e. fats) are energy giving foods. The other options, i.e. iodised salt and spinach are good sources of iodine and iron, respectively.

Q. 5 Read the following statements about diseases.

    (i) They are caused by germs.

    (ii) They are caused due to the lack of nutrients in our diet.

    (iii) They can be passed on to another person through contact.

    (iv) They can be prevented by taking a balanced diet.

Which pair of statements best describes a deficiency disease?

    (a) (i) and (ii)   (b) (ii) and (iii)   (c) (ii) and (iv)   (d) (i) and (iii)

Ans. *(c)* Deficiency disease is a disease which arises due to the lack of nutrients in our diet over a long period of time, e.g. Scurvy, kwashiorkor.

To prevent these diseases, it is essential to have a balanced diet. It is a diet, which contains adequate amounts of all the nutrients as well as sufficient quantity of water and roughage.

Q. 6 Given below are the steps to test the presence of proteins in a food item.

    I. Take a small quantity of the food item in a test tube, add 10 drops of water to it and shake it.

    II. Make a paste or powder of food to be tested.

    III. Add 10 drops of caustic soda solution to the test tube and shake well.

    IV. Add 2 drops of copper sulphate solution to it.

Which of the following is the correct sequence of the steps?

    (a) I, II, IV, III   (b) II, I, IV, III   (c) II, I, III, IV   (d) IV, II, I, III

Ans. *(b)* The presence of proteins in a food material is tested on the basis of a reaction between proteins and alkaline solution of copper sulphate, that gives a voilet colour.

The test involves the following steps in sequences II, I, IV, III.

Very Short Answer Type Questions

Q. 7 Unscramble the following words related to components of food and write them in the space provided.

    (a) reinpot ....   (b) menliars ....

    (c) tivanmi...........   (d) bocatradhyer ....

    (e) nitesturn...........   (f) tfa ....

Ans. (a) Protein   (b) Minerals

     (c) Vitamin   (d) Carbohydrate

     (e) Nutrients   (f) Fat

Q. 8 Which of the following food item does not provide any nutrient?

Milk, Water, Orange juice, Tomato soup

Ans. Among the given food items, **water** does not provide any nutrient, but is needed by our body for various functions such as transport of digested food, controlling and regulating body temperature, etc.

The other food items, i.e. milk provides proteins, fats and vitamins, while orange juice and tomato soup provide vitamin-C.

Short Answer Type Questions

Q. 9 Fill in the blanks from the list of words given below

(carbohydrate, fat, protein, starch, sugar, vitamin–A, vitamin–C, roughage, balanced diet, obesity, goitre)

(a) Egg yolk is rich in ...... and egg albumin is rich in ....

(b) Deficiency dieseases can be prevented by taking a ....

(c) Eating too much of fat rich foods may lead to a condition called ....

(d) The component of food that does not provide any nutrient to our body and yet is essential in our food is ....

(e) The vitamin that gets easily destroyed by heating during cooking is ....

Ans. (a) fat; protein   (b) balanced diet   (c) obesity   (d) roughage

(e) vitamin-C

Q. 10 Read the items of food listed below. Classify them into carbohydrate rich, protein rich and fat rich foods and fill them in the given table.

Mung dal, fish, mustard oil, sweet potato, milk, rice, egg, beans, butter, butter milk (chhachh), cottage cheese (paneer), peas, maize, white bread.

Carbohydrate rich food item	Protein rich food item	Fat rich food item
....	....	....
....	....	....

Ans. The completely filled table is as given below :

Carbohydrate rich food items (A)	Protein rich food items (B)	Fat rich food items (C)
Sweet potato	Mung dal	Mustard oil
Rice	Fish	Milk
Maize	Milk	Egg
White bread	Egg	Butter
	Beans	
	Butter milk	
	Cottage cheese	
	Peas	

Q. 11 Tasty food is not always nutritious and nutritious food may not always be tasty to eat. Comment with examples.

Ans. Tasty food is not always nutritious and nutritious food may not always be tasty to eat. This is true as the junk and processed food is tasty and is made to be addictive, but is unhealthy. Certain examples in favour of the above statement are:

(i) Potato chips are tasty to eat but not nutritious as they contain huge amount of fats.

(ii) Green leafy vegetables either boiled or steamed are very nutritious but not good in taste.

(iii) Certain fast foods like pizza, burger, etc., are very good in taste but are not nutritious as they contain huge amount of fat.

Q. 12 While using iodine in the laboratory, some drops of iodine fell on Paheli's socks and some fell on her teacher's saree. The drops of iodine on the saree turned blue-black, while their colour did not change on the socks. What can be the possible reason?

Ans. The drops of iodine are used to detect the presence of starch, by appearance of blue-black colour. The possible reason for blue-black colour on teacher's saree could be the presence of starch. The saree might have been starched. Paheli's socks did not have starch on it, therefore their colour did not change.

Q. 13 Paheli and Boojho peeled some potatoes and cut them into small pieces. They washed and boiled them in water. They threw away the excess water and fried them in oil adding salt and spices. Although the potato dish tasted very good, its nutrient value was less. Suggest a method of cooking potatoes that will not lower the nutrients in them.

Ans. Methods of cooking potatoes that will not lower the nutrient content are as follows:

(i) Washing of potato after it has been peeled and cut, removes the water-soluble vitamins and some minerals from it. So, it should be first washed and then peeled and cut.

(ii) The excess water in which the potatoes were boiled should not be thrown away as it leads to loss of some of the proteins and minerals. This should be avoided.

(iii) A small amount of water and small quantity of oil should be used for cooking as it conserves the nutrients.

Q. 14 Paheli avoids eating vegetables but likes to eat biscuits, noodles and white bread. She frequently complains of stomachache and constipation. What are the food items that she should include in her diet to get rid of the problem? Give reason for your answer.

Ans. Paheli seems to lack roughage in her diet. Roughage is the fibrous matter in food which cannot be digested. It has no nutritive value but its presence is essential for normal functioning of the digestive system.

Therefore, Paheli must include whole grains, pulses, fresh fruits and vegetables in her diet as fibre (roughage) is found in these food items.

Q. 15 (a) List all those components of food that provide nutrients.

(b) Mention two components of food that do not provide nutrients.

Ans. (a) Components of food that provide nutrients are **carbohydrates, fats, proteins, vitamins and minerals**. Of these, carbohydrates and fats provide energy, proteins are needed for growth and repair, vitamins help in protecting against diseases and minerals assist in proper functioning, normal growth and good health.

(b) Two components of food that do not provide nutrients are **water** and **roughage** (dietary fibre). Water is needed for various functions such as transport of digested food, to excrete waste products and roughage is needed for normal working of digestive system.

Q. 16 'Minerals and vitamins are needed in very small quantities by our body as compared to other components, yet they are an important part of a balanced diet'. Explain the statement.

Ans. Minerals and vitamins though are needed in very small quantities by our body, but are important part of balanced diet because

(i) Vitamins help in protecting our body against diseases. These are necessary for good eyesight (vitamin-A), growth (vitamin-B_1), keeping teeth gums and joints healthy (vitamin-C) and normal growth of bones and teeth (vitamin-D).

(ii) Minerals are needed in our body for building bones and teeth (calcium and phosphorus), formation of blood (iron), coagulation of blood and functioning of muscles (calcium) and functioning of thyroid gland (iron). Thus, assist in proper functioning normal growth and good health.

Q. 17 'Water does not provide nutrients, yet it is an important component of food'. Explain.

Ans. Water does not provide nutrients, yet it is an important component of food because it helps

(i) to transport digested food to body cells.

(ii) to absorb nutrients from the food.

(iii) to get rid of waste products from the body.

(iv) to control and regulate the body temperature.

Long Answer Type Questions

Q. 18 Boojho was having difficulty in seeing things in dim light. The doctor tested his eyesight and prescribed a particular vitamin supplement. He also advised him to include a few food items in his diet.

(a) Which deficiency disease is he suffering from?

(b) Which food component may be lacking in his diet?

(c) Suggest some food items that he should include in his diet. (any four)

Ans. (a) Boojho is suffering from night blindness.

(b) The food component which may be lacking in his diet is vitamin-A.

(c) The food items that he should include in his diet to overcome the deficiency of vitamin-A are green vegetables, carrot, papaya, milk, mango and fish liver oil.

Q. 19 Solve the crossword puzzle given as figure from the clues given below.

Across

1. Lack of nutrients in our diet over a long period causes these diseases. (10)
2. Rice and potato are rich in this type of carbohydrate. (6)
3. Deficiency disease in bones making it becomes soft and bent. (7)
4. The diet that provides all the nutrients that our body needs in right quantities along with adequate amount of roughage and water. (8, 4)
5. Deficiency disease with bleeding gums. (6)
6. Disease caused due to the deficiency of iodine. (6)

Down

7. Starch and sugar in our food are rich in this type of energy giving nutrient. (13)
8. The term given to the useful components of food. (9)
9. The disease caused by deficiency of iron in diet. (7)
10. Green leafy vegetables and apples are rich in this mineral. (4)
11. Deficiency disease caused due to the lack of vitamin-B$_1$ in the diet. (8)

Ans. **Across**

1. DEFICIENCY   2. STARCH
3. RICKETS   4. BALANCED DIET
5. SCURVY   6. GOITRE

Down

7. CARBOHYDRATES   8. NUTRIENTS

9. ANAEMIA   10. IRON

11. BERI-BERI

Q. 20 Observe the items given in the figure carefully and answer the questions that follow.

(a) Food item rich in carbohydrates is ...... (i) ....

(b) Egg is a rich source of protein, the mineral ...... (ii) ...... and vitamin .... (iii) ....

(c) .... (iv) .... is a rich source of fat.

(d) Milk provides ... (v) ..., vitamin-D and ... (vi) ... (mineral).

(e) ... (vii) ... (fruit) is a rich source of vitamin-A.

(f) Spinach is a good source of the mineral ... (viii) ... .

(g) Both eggs and ... (ix) ... are rich in ... (x) ... .

Ans. In the given diagram,

(a) Chapatties (i)

(b) Calcium (ii); Vitamins-D, B_{12} (iii)

(c) Butter (iv)

(d) Protein (v); Calcium (vi)

(e) Papaya (vii)

(f) Iron (viii)

(g) Peas (ix); proteins (x)

Q. 21 Snakes and Ladders

Make a board game just like snakes and ladders with 10×10 grid boxes.

The mouth of the snake will represent the faulty food habit or faulty method of cooking. Its tail will represent the deficiency disease caused or loss of any nutrient in food.

Similarly, the box at the base of a ladder will represent healthy food habit or healthy method of cooking.

Its upper end will represent the beneficial effect of that habit. An example is given as figure. Complete the board and play with your friends.

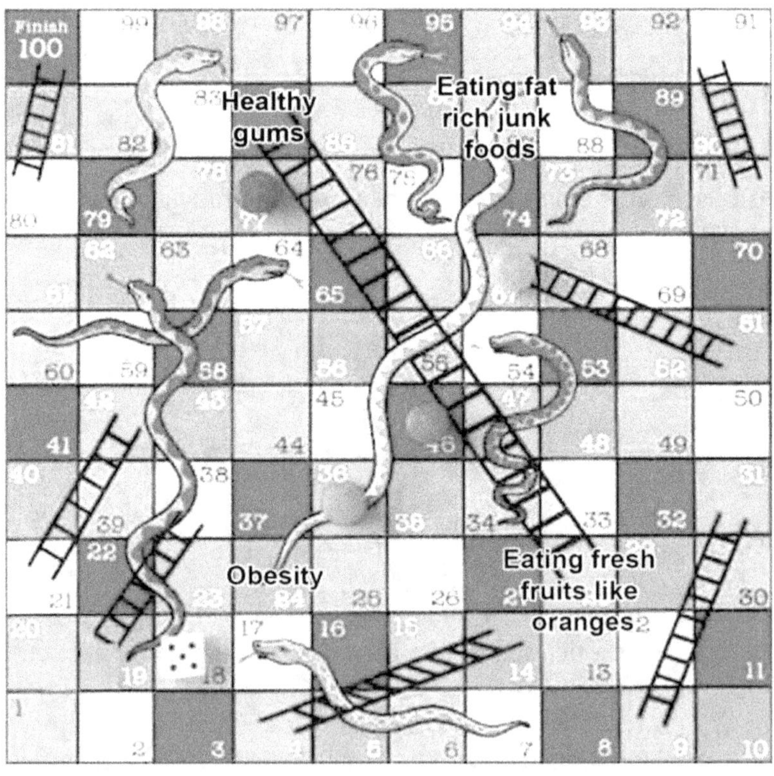

Ans. The solved Snakes and Ladders is given below:

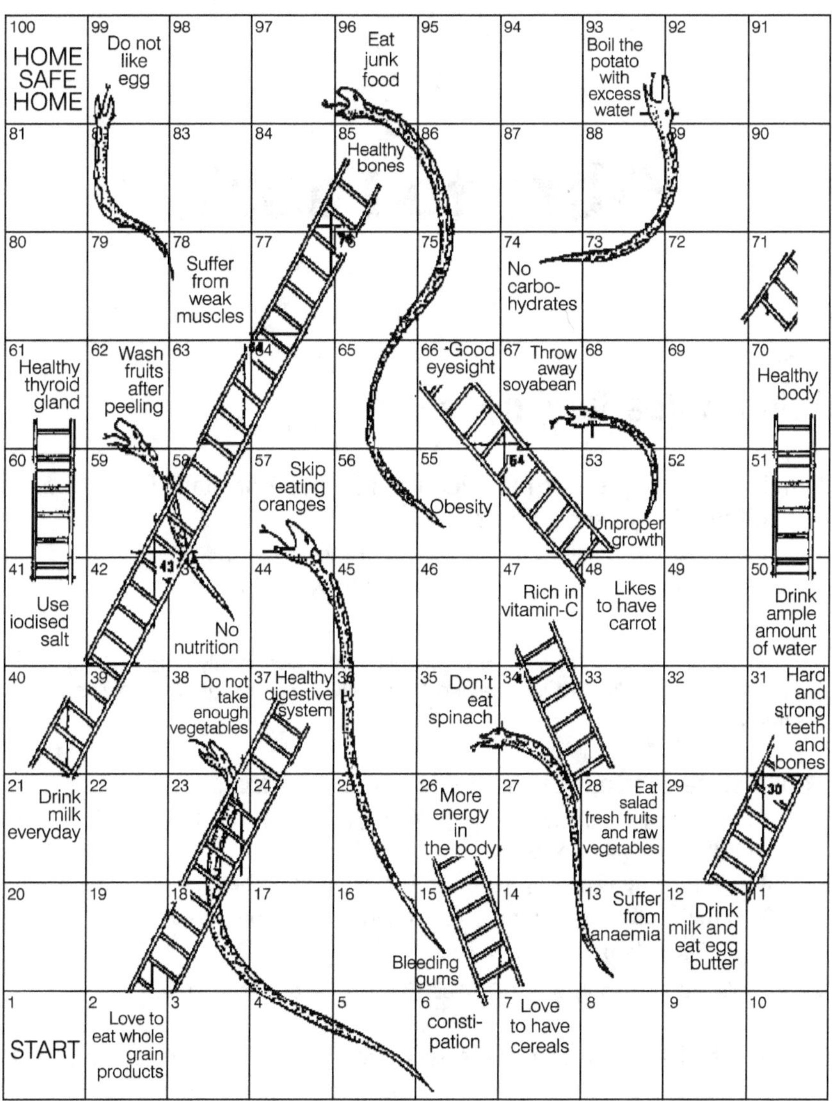

3

Fibre to Fabric

Multiple Choice Questions (MCQs)

Q. 1 Paheli wants to present her friend a gift made of plant fibre. Which out of the following will she select?

    (a) Jute bag   (b) Woollen shawl

    (c) Silk saree   (d) Nylon scarf

Ans. *(a)* Jute bag

Jute bag is made up of plant fibre. Wool is most commonly obtained from sheep (animal fibre). Silk fibre is obtained from silkworm (animal fibre). Nylon is a synthetic fibre.

Q. 2 Which statement out of the following is incorrect?

    (a) Use of charkha was popularised by Mahatma Gandhi as a part of the Independence movement

    (b) In India, jute is mainly grown in Kerala and Punjab

    (c) To make fabric, the fibres are first converted into yarns

    (d) Sufi Saint Kabir was a weaver

Ans. *(b)* In India, jute is mainly grown in West Bengal, Bihar and Assam.

Q. 3 Which of the following materials did people use in ancient times for making clothes?

    (i) Leaves of trees

    (ii) Newspaper

    (iii) Metal foils

    (iv) Animal skins and furs

    (a) (i) and (ii)   (b) (i) and (iii)

    (c) (ii) and (iii)   (d) (i) and (iv)

Ans. *(d)* (i) and (iv)

In ancient times, people used the bark and big leaves of trees or animal skins and furs to cover themselves.

Q. 4 Which of the following is not a natural fibre?

    (a) Cotton   (b) Jute   (c) Nylon   (d) Flax

Ans. *(c)* Nylon

Cotton, flax and jute are the natural fibres obtained from plants. Nylon is a synthetic fibre.

Q. 5 Which set of substances is not used for making fibres?

    (a) Silk, chemicals   (b) Yak hair, camel hair

    (c) Husk, bones   (d) Flax, wool

Ans. *(c)* Husk and bones are not used for making fibres.

Substances in options (a), (b) and (d) are used for making fibres.

Q. 6 Boojho went to a cloth shop. There he found a fabric which was smooth to touch, had vibrant colour and shine. The fabric could be

    (a) cotton   (b) wool

    (c) silk   (d) jute

Ans. *(c)* Silk fibre is smooth to touch, has vibrant colour and shine. Cotton is light and reasonable smooth. Wool is fluffy and jute is rough.

Q. 7 Which part of the jute plant is used for getting jute fibre?

    (a) Flower   (b) Stem

    (c) Fruit   (d) Leaf

Ans. *(b)* Jute fibre is obtained from the stem of the jute plant.

Q. 8 Yarn is woven to get fabric using

    (a) charkha   (b) spinning machines

    (c) looms   (d) knitting needles

Ans. *(c)* The weaving of yarn to make fabrics is done by using 'looms'.

Loom is a device used for making fabrics by weaving yarn or threads.

Q. 9 Beera is a farmer. His field has black soil and the climate is warm. Which fibre yielding plant should he grow in his field?

    (a) Jute   (b) Cotton

    (c) Coconut   (d) Wool

Ans. *(b)* Cotton fibre comes from the cotton plants and cotton crop is usually grown at places having black soil and warm climate. So, Beera should grow cotton plant in his field.

Q. 10 The correct sequence to get cloth is

    (a) fibre → fabric → yarn   (b) fibre → yarn → fabric

    (c) fabric → yarn → fibre   (d) yarn → fibre → fabric

Ans. *(b)* The correct sequence to get cloth is fibre → yarn → fabric.

    (i) Fibres are first converted to yarn by the process of spinning.

    (ii) Fabric is made from yarn by the process of weaving or knitting.

Q. 11 Boojho wants to make yarn from fibre at home. Which of the following will he use to carry out the task?

    (a) Powerloom   (b) Handloom

    (c) Charkha   (d) Knitting needles

Ans. *(c)* Hand operated device which is used for spinning cotton and making yarn is spinning wheel or charkha. So, Boojho will use charkha to make yarn from fibre at home.

Very Short Answer Type Questions

Q. 12 Yarn, fabric and fibres are related to each other. Show the relationship by filling the blanks in the following sentence.

Fabric of cotton saree is made by weaving cotton .... which in turn is made by spinning thin cotton ....

Ans. yarn, fibres

Q. 13 Some terms related to fabrics are jumbled up and given below. Write them in their correct form.

    (a) Onttoc   (b) Sinnping   (c) Vingwea   (d) Bisref

Ans. The correct form is given below :

    (a) Cotton   (b) Spinning

    (c) Weaving   (d) Fibres

Q. 14 State whether the following statements are true or false. If false, correct them

    (a) Silk is a plant fibre.

    (b) Jute is obtained from the leaves of a plant.

    (c) Weaving is a process of arranging two sets of yarns together.

    (d) Cotton yarn on burning gives an odour similar to that of a burning paper.

Ans. (a) False,

      Silk is a animal fibre which is obtained from silkworm.

    (b) False,

      Jute is obtained from the stem of a jute plant.

    (c) True

    (d) True

Q. 15 The following is an answer given by Boojho to a question asked by his teacher–"cotton, wool, silk and jute are classified as natural fibres whereas nylon and polyester are classified as synthetic fibres."

Can you tell what question the teacher has asked?

Ans. The teacher has asked, the following type of question,

Classify the following fibres as natural and synthetic.

Polyester, jute, wool, nylon, silk, cotton.

Q. 16 Once, Paheli visited a tailor shop and brought home some cuttings of fabric to study their properties. She took two pieces and found that one of the pieces was shrinking when it was burnt with a candle. However, the other did not shrink on burning. Can you help her to find out which of the two was a cotton fabric and which was a silk fabric?

Ans. If a piece of cloth shrinks on burning, then the fabric is silk and the other fabric is cotton because cotton fabric does not shrinks on burning.

Q. 17 One way of making fabric from yarn is weaving, what is the other?

Ans. Knitting is the other way of making fabrics from yarn. In knitting, a fabric is made by interlocking loops of single yarn with knitting needles or machines.

Short Answer Type Questions

Q. 18 Boojho with perfect eyesight was finding it difficult to pass a thread through the eye of a needle. What can be the possible reason for this?

Ans. If it is difficult to pass a thread through the eye of a needle then it is possible that the end of the thread may be separated into a few thin strands or the thread may be quite thick.

Q. 19 In ancient times, stitching was not known. People used to simply drape the fabrics around different parts of their body. Even, today a number of unstitched fabrics are used by both men and women. Can you give four such examples of clothes?

Ans. Saree, dhoti, lungi, turban, dupatta, towel, etc are the examples of such clothes.

Q. 20 Match articles given in Column I with the articles of Column II.

	Column I		Column II
(a)	Sweater	(i)	Cotton
(b)	Cotton bolls	(ii)	Wool
(c)	Dhoti	(iii)	Ginning
(d)	Gunny bags	(iv)	Jute

Ans. The correct matching is as given

(a)—(ii), (b)—(iii), (c)—(i), (d)—(iv)

Q. 21 Fill in the blanks to complete the life story of cotton fibre.

My parents, cotton plants were grown in .... soil and .... climate. The plants bore fruits called .... I, the cotton fibre was separated from seeds in the cotton bolls by the process of .... Other cotton fibres and myself were made into yarn by the process of .... The yarn was .... to give beautiful colours and then .... to get cotton fabric.

Ans. black, warm, cotton bolls, ginning, spinning, dyed, woven

Q. 22 Match the terms given in Column I with the statements given in Column II.

	Column I		Column II
(a)	Weaving	(i)	A single yarn used to make fabric
(b)	Knitting	(ii)	Combing of cotton fibres to remove
(c)	Spinning	(iii)	Yarns are made from these thin strands
(d)	Ginning	(iv)	These are spun from fibres and then used to make fabrics
(e)	Fibre	(v)	Process of arranging two sets of yarns together to make a fabric
(f)	Yarn	(vi)	Process of making yarn from fibres

Ans. The correct matching is as given

(a)—(v), (b)—(i), (c)—(vi), (d)—(ii), (e)—(iii), (f)—(iv)

Q. 23 Fill in the names of useful items made from jute fibres in the following figure. One such example is given.

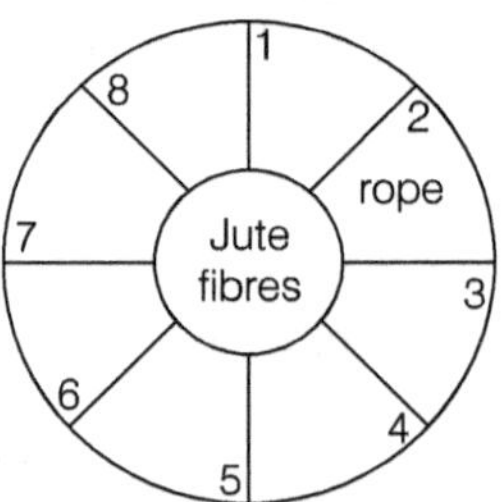

Ans. The name of useful items made from jute fibres in the given figure is as below:

Long Answer Type Questions

Q. 24 A cotton shirt, before it reaches you, completes a long journey. Elaborate this journey starting from cotton bolls.

Ans. Cotton is the most important in all plant fibres, used to make clothes. Cotton shirt can be prepared by following steps:

Cotton bolls $\xrightarrow{\text{Ginning}}$ Cotton fibre $\xrightarrow{\text{Spinning}}$ Cotton yarn $\xrightarrow{\text{Weaving}}$ Cotton fabric $\xrightarrow{\text{Sewing}}$ Cotton shirt

The making of cotton shirt is a long process. From cotton bolls, cotton is usually picked up from the plants in the fields usually by hand. Fibres are then separated from the seeds by combing. This process is called ginning.

In spinning processes, the fibres from a mass of cotton wool are drawn out and twisted. This brings the fibres together to form a long and twisted thread called 'yarn'.

In weaving process, cotton fabric is made by arranging two sets of cotton yarns at right angles to one another. Weaving is done on looms. Now, on sewing this cotton fabric by needle on sewing machine we get the cotton shirt.

Q. 25 Describe the two main processes of making fabric from yarn.

Ans. The two main processes of making fabric from yarn are weaving and knitting.

Weaving It is a process of making fabric (or cloth) by arranging two sets of yarns passing in one direction with other yarns at right angle to them.

In other words, two sets of yarns are woven to make a fabric. Weaving of fabric is done on looms. The looms are either hand operated or power operated.

Knitting It is a process of making a fabric by interlocking loops of single yarn with knitting needles or machines.

Knitting fabrics are made of a single yarn running throughout the fabric. Socks and many other clothing items are made of knitted fabrics.

4

Sorting Materials and Groups

Multiple Choice Questions (MCQs)

Q. 1 An iron nail is kept in each of the following liquids. In which case would it lose its shine and appear dull?

    (a) Mustard oil   (b) Soft drink
    (c) Coconut oil   (d) Kerosene

Ans. *(b)* An iron nail kept in soft drink would lose its shine and appear dull became soft drink contains carbonic acid which reacts with iron nail, so it gives dull appearance.

Iron nail has no reaction with mustard oil, coconut oil and kerosene, so does not lose its shine, when kept in these solutions.

Q. 2 Pick one material from the following which is completely soluble in water.

    (a) Chalk powder   (b) Tea leaves
    (c) Glucose   (d) Sawdust

Ans. *(c)* Glucose is completely soluble in water because its particles are so small and spread uniformly in water that we cannot see them. But chalk powder, tea leaves and sawdust are insoluble in water and settle down at the bottom of the container.

Q. 3 You are provided with the following materials:

    (i) Magnifying glass   (ii) Mirror
    (iii) Stainless steel plate   (iv) Glass tumbler

Which of the above materials will you identify as transparent?

    (a) (i) and (ii)   (b) (i) and (iii)
    (c) (i) and (iv)   (d) (iii) and (iv)

Ans. *(c)* Through magnifying glass and glass tumbler we can see the objects clearly so these materials are transparent.

Q. 4 Boojho found a bag containing the following materials:

    (i) Mirror

    (ii) Paper stained with oil

    (iii) Magnet

    (iv) Glass spectacles

Help Boojho in finding out the material(s) which is/are opaque.

    (a) Only (i)   (b) Only (iv)

    (c) (i) and (iii)   (d) (ii) and (iv)

Ans. *(c)* Mirror and magnet are opaque materials because we cannot see through these materials. Paper stained with oil is translucent material and glass spectacles is transparent.

Q. 5 While doing an activity in class, the teacher asked Paheli to handover a translucent material. Which among the following materials will Paheli pick and give her teacher?

    (a) Glass tumbler   (b) Mirror

    (c) Muslin cloth   (d) Aluminium foil

Ans. *(c)* The material through which an object can be seen but not clearly is called translucent. Hence, muslin cloth is a translucent material. Mirror and aluminium foil are opaque and glass tumbler is transparent material.

Q. 6 Which pair of substances among the following would float in a tumbler half-filled with water?

    (a) Cotton thread, thermocol

    (b) Feather, plastic ball

    (c) Pin, oil drops

    (d) Rubber band, coin

Ans. *(b)* All the materials, which are lighter than water, float on water here feather and plastic ball. Among the given pair of substances which would float in a tumbler half-filled with water.

Q. 7 Which among the following are commonly used for making a safety pin?

    (a) Wood and glass   (b) Plastic and glass

    (c) Leather and plastic   (d) Steel and plastic

Ans. *(d)* Wood, glass and leather materials cannot be used for making safety pin. Steel and plastic are commonly used for making a safety pin.

Q. 8 Which of the following materials is not lustrous?

    (a) Gold   (b) Silver

    (c) Wood   (d) Diamond

Ans. *(c)* Gold, silver and diamond have shiny appearance are said to have luster. Wood has dull appearance, so wood is not lustrous.

Q. 9 Which of the following statements is not true?

    (a) Materials are grouped for convenience

    (b) Materials are grouped to study their properties

    (c) Materials are grouped for fun

    (d) Materials are grouped according to their uses

Ans. *(c)* Materials are grouped for our convenience and to make it convenient to study their properties. Materials are also grouped according to their uses.

So, only statement (c) is not true.

Q. 10 Find the odd one out from the following.

    (a) Tawa   (b) Spade

    (c) Pressure cooker   (d) Eraser

Ans. *(d)* Tawa, spade and pressure cooker are all hard materials i.e. cannot be easily compressed, cut, bent (moulded) or scratched but eraser can be easily cut, bent or scratched. So, the odd one is eraser.

Q. 11 Which type of the following materials is used for making the front glass (wind screen) of a car?

    (a) Transparent   (b) Translucent

    (c) Opaque   (d) All of these

Ans. *(a)* Transparent material is used for making the front glass (wind screen) of a car.

Very Short Answer Type Questions

Q. 12 It was Paheli's birthday. Her grandmother gave her two gifts made up of metals, one old dull silver spoon and a pair of lustrous gold ear-rings. She was surprised to see the difference in the appearance of the two metals. Can you explain the reason for this difference?

Ans. Gold metal does not lose its shine or luster when exposed to atmosphere. So gold ornaments look new even after several years of use. Actually, gold metal is highly unreactive metal which remains unaffected by air, water and other gases in the atmosphere whereas silver metal on long exposure to moist air loses its shine and becomes dull. That why old silver spoon was giving dull appearance.

Q. 13 Mixtures of red chilli powder in water, butter in water, petrol in water and honey in water were given to Radha, Sudha, Sofia and Raveena, respectively. Whose mixture is in solution form?

Ans. Raveena has got a solution because honey will dissolve in water whereas red chilli powder, butter and petrol float on water.

Q. 14 On a bright sunny day, Shikha was playing hide and seek with her brother. She hid herself behind a glass door. Do you think her brother will be able to locate her? If yes, why? If no, why not?

Ans. Yes, her brother can easily locate her because glass door is a transparent material. The transparent materials allow almost all the light to pass through them due to which the object or person behind them can be seen clearly.

Q. 15 Take a small cotton boll and place it in a tumbler/bowl filled with water. Observe it for at least 10 minutes. Will it float or sink in water and why?

Ans. Cotton boll initially floats on water but after few minutes (i.e. 10 min), it sinks because it absorbs water.

Short Answer Type Questions

Q. 16 Which among the following materials would you identify as soft materials and why?
Ice, rubber band, leaf, eraser, pencil, pearl, a piece of wooden board, cooked rice, pulses and fresh chapatti.

Ans. Materials which can be compressed, cut, bent (moulded) or scratched easily are called soft materials. Rubber band, leaf, eraser, cooked rice and fresh chapati are soft materials because they can be compressed, cut, bent or scratched easily.

Q. 17 You are provided with the following materials: Turmeric, honey, mustard oil, water, glucose, rice flour, groundnut oil.
Make any three pairs of substances where one substance is soluble in the other and any three pairs of substances where one substance remains insoluble in the other substance.

Ans. Substances which are soluble :
  (i) Honey in water
  (ii) Glucose in water
  (iii) Groundnut oil in mustard oil
Substances which are insoluble :
  (i) Turmeric in water
  (ii) Rice flour in water
  (iii) Mustard oil in water

Q. 18 During summer holidays, a group of children collected a lump of salt, green grass, broken glass piece, a small thermocol box, pen, iron nail, glass marbles, hair, naphthalene ball, a piece of sugar candy (mishri) and tried to group them on the basis of properties given in table. Help them in filling the table.

Name of the material	Appearance (Hard/Soft)	Transparency (Transparent/ Translucent/ Opaque)	Floats/Sinks in water	Soluble/ Insoluble in water
....	....	....	....	....
....	....	....	....	....

Ans. The complete table is shown as below :

Name of the material	Appearance (Hard/Soft)	Transparency (Transparent/ Translucent/ Opaque)	Floats/Sinks in water	Soluble/ Insoluble in water
Lump of salt	Hard	Opaque	Sinks	Soluble
Green grass	Soft	Opaque	Floats	Insoluble
Broken glass piece	Hard	Transparent	Sinks	Insoluble
A small thermocol box	Soft	Opaque	Floats	Insoluble
Pen	Hard	Opaque	Sinks	Insoluble
Iron nail	Hard	Opaque	Sinks	Insoluble
Glass marbles	Hard	Transparent	Sinks	Insoluble
Hair	Soft	Opaque	Floats	Insoluble
Naphthalene ball	Hard	Opaque	Sinks	Insoluble
A piece of sugar candy (mishri)	Hard	Translucent	Sinks	Soluble

Q. 19 Arrange the jumbled words to arrive at the appropriate names of materials and also write two uses of each.

    (a) Milaunuim   (b) Tcaslpi

    (c) Soekrnee   (d) Gavnier

Ans. Arrangement of the words and their uses are as follows:

    (a) **Aluminium** It is used in foil, aircrafts, etc.

    (b) **Plastic** It is used in making bucket, pencil box, etc.

    (c) **Kerosene** It is used as a fuel, solvent, etc.

    (d) **Vinegar** It is used in food ingredient, preservative, etc

Q. 20 Match the objects given in Column I with the materials given in Column II.

	Column I		Column II
(a)	Surgical instruments	(i)	Plastic
(b)	Newspaper	(ii)	Animal product
(c)	Electrical switches	(iii)	Steel
(d)	Wool	(iv)	Plant product

Ans. The correct matching is as given:

    (a)—(iii),   (b)—(iv),   (c)—(i),   (d)—(ii)

    Note *(a) Surgical instruments are made up of steel.*

        (b) Newspaper is made up of paper and paper is obtained from plants.

        (c) Electrical switches are made up of plastic.

        (d) Wool is obtained from wool yielding animals so wool is animal product.

Q. 21 Crossword Puzzle Pick five objects from the word box given as figure, which are opaque and would sink in water.

O	S	T	P	L	E
A	T	L	E	E	R
C	O	I	N	A	A
O	N	K	C	F	S
A	E	E	I	W	E
L	L	Y	L	R	R

Ans. Name of the objects, which are opaque and would sink in water are :

(i) Coal

(iii) Pencil

(v) Coin

(ii) Stone

(iv) Eraser

O	S	T	P	L	E
A	T	L	E	E	R
C	O	I	N	A	A
O	N	K	C	F	S
A	E	E	I	W	E
L	L	Y	L	R	R

Note *All these objects are heavier than water so these objects would sink in water.*

Long Answer Type Questions

Q. 22 Chalk, iron nail, wood, aluminium, candle, cotton usually look different from each other. Give some properties by which we can prove that these materials are different.

Ans. We can differentiate these materials on the basis of lustre, hardness, softness, roughness or smoothness.

Material	Properties
Chalk	Rough on the surface, cannot be compressed
Iron nail	Shine (lustre), hard
Aluminium	Shine (lustre), hard
Wood	Hard to compress, dull appearance
Candle	Soft to compress
Cotton	Soft to compress

Q. 23 Why do you think oxygen dissolved in water is important for the survival of aquatic animals and plants.

Ans. Oxygen gas dissolves in water i.e. oxygen gas is soluble in water. The plants and animals which live in water use the oxygen dissolved in water for respiration. Thus, oxygen gas dissolved in water is very important for the survival of animals and plants that live in water.

Q. 24 Differentiate among opaque, translucent and transparent materials, giving one example of each.

Ans. **Opaque** Those materials through which we cannot see at all are called opaque materials, e.g. Car board.

Translucent Those materials through which we cannot see clearly are called translucent materials. e.g. Butter paper.

Transparent Those materials through which we can see clearly are called transparent materials e.g. Glass.

Q. 25 Sugar, salt, mustard oil, sand, sawdust, honey, chalk powder, petals of flower, soil, copper sulphate crystals, glucose, wheat flour are some substances given to Paheli. She wants to know whether these substances are soluble in water or not. Help her in identifying soluble and insoluble substances in water.

Ans. Substances which completely dissolve in water are soluble in water.

Substances soluble in water are sugar, salt, honey, copper sulphate crystals, glucose.

Substances which does not dissolve in water are insoluble in water. Substances insoluble in water are mustard oil, sand, sawdust, chalk powder, petals of flower, soil, wheat flour.

5

Separation of Substances

Multiple Choice Questions (MCQs)

Q. 1 Paheli bought some vegetables such as french beans, lady's finger, green chillies, brinjals and potatoes all mixed in a bag. Which of the following methods of separation would be most appropriate for her to separate them?

    (a) Winnowing   (b) Sieving

    (c) Threshing   (d) Hand-picking

Ans. *(d)* Hand-picking method would be most appropriate for her to separate vegetables because vegetables can be picked up easily by hand one by one, and can be separated.

Q. 2 Boojho's grandmother is suffering from diabetes. Her doctor advised her to take 'lassi' with less fat content. Which of the following methods would be most appropriate for Boojho to prepare it?

    (a) Filtration   (b) Decantation

    (c) Churning   (d) Winnowing

Ans. *(c)* Churning is the method by which cream (fat content) from the milk is separated. So, he should prepare 'Lassi' by the process churning.

Q. 3 Which of the following mixtures would you be able to separate using the method of filtration?

    (a) Oil in water   (b) Cornflakes in milk

    (c) Salt in water   (d) Sugar in milk

Ans. *(b)* Filtration method is used for separating insoluble substance from a liquid. But mixture of two liquids such as oil in water cannot be separated by this method. Also salt in water and sugar in milk are completely dissolved so, cannot be separated by filtration. So, cornflakes in milk can be separated by filtration.

Q. 4 Which amongst the following methods would be most appropriate to separate grains from bundles of stalks?

    (a) Hand-picking   (b) Winnowing
    (c) Sieving   (d) Threshing

Ans. *(d)* The grains are separated from stalks (on which they grow) by the process of threshing. In this process stalks (of wheat, paddy, etc) are beaten to separate grains from the bundle of stalks.

> **Note** *This method is based on the fact that the stalks (or stems) of the crop plant are soft material whereas the grains themselves are very hard. Being soft, stalks can be broken into pieces on beating but the grains remains unaffected.*

Q. 5 Four mixtures are given below:

    (i) Kidney beans and chickpeas
    (ii) Pulses and rice
    (iii) Riceflakes and corn
    (iv) Potato wafers and biscuits

Which of these can be separated by the method of winnowing?

    (a) (i) and (ii)   (b) (ii) and (iii)
    (c) (i) and (iii)   (d) (iii) and (iv)

Ans. *(d)* Winnowing is used to separate heavier and lighter components of a mixture by wind or by blowing air. Rice flakes and potato wafers are lighter substances in the mixture, so these are separated from the given mixture by winnowing.

Q. 6 While preparing chapattis, Paheli found that the flour to be used was mixed with wheat grains. Which out of the following is the most suitable method to separate the grains from the flour?

    (a) Threshing   (b) Sieving
    (c) Winnowing   (d) Filtration

Ans. *(b)* The most suitable method to separate the grains from the flour is by sieving. Sieving is used to separate those solid mixture which have components of different sizes.

Q. 7 You might have observed the preparation of ghee from butter and cream at home. Which method(s) can be used to separate ghee from the residue?

    (i) Evaporation   (ii) Decantation
    (iii) Filtration   (iv) Churning

Which of the following combinations is the correct answer?

    (a) (i) and (ii)   (b) (ii) and (iii)
    (c) (ii) and (iv)   (d) Only (iv)

Ans. *(b)* By decantation and then by filtration ghee can be separated from the residue.

> **Note** *Decantation is the process of pouring out the liquid without disturbing the sediment.*

Q. 8 In an activity, a teacher dissolved a small amount of solid copper sulphate in a tumbler half-filled with water. Which method would you use to get back solid copper sulphate from the solution?

    (a) Decantation   (b) Evaporation

    (c) Sedimentation   (d) Condensation

Ans. *(b)* By the process of evaporation we can get back solid copper sulphate from the solution. The process of evaporation for separating a mixture is based on the fact that liquids vaporise easily whereas solids do not vaporise easily.

Q. 9 During summer, Boojho carries water in a transparent plastic bottle to his school. One day, he left his bottle in the school. The bottle still had some water left in it. The next day, he observed some water droplets on the inner surface of the empty portion of the bottle. These droplets of water were formed due to

    (a) boiling and condensation

    (b) evaporation and saturation

    (c) evaporation and condensation

    (d) condensation and saturation

Ans. *(c)* The droplets of water on the inner surface of bottle were formed due to evaporation and condensation.

    Note *The process of conversion of water vapour into liquid form is called condensation.*

Q. 10 Paheli asked for a glass of water from Boojho. He gave her a glass of ice cold water. Paheli observed some water droplets on the outer surface of the glass and asked Boojho, how these droplets of water were formed? Which of the following should be Boojho's answer?

    (a) Evaporation of water from the glass

    (b) Water that seeped out from the glass

    (c) Evaporation of atmospheric water vapour

    (d) Condensation of atmospheric water vapour

Ans. *(d)* Water droplets on the outer surface of glass is formed due to condensation of atmospheric water vapour. Actually the water vapour present in air, on coming in contact with the cold glass of water, loses energy and gets converted to liquid state, which we see as water droplets.

Very Short Answer Type Questions

Q. 11 Sheela, Saima and Ravi have to dissolve maximum amount of sugar in the same amount of milk, so as to win in a game. Ravi took hot boiling milk, while Saima took ice cold milk. Sheela managed to get milk at room temperature. Whom do you think would win the game and why?

Ans. Ravi would win the game because Ravi took hot boiling milk and hot milk at higher temperature would dissolve more amount of sugar and also solubility increases with temperature. So, Ravi would be able to dissolve maximum amount of sugar in milk.

Q. 12 Fill in the blanks.

    (i) Small pieces of stones can be removed from rice by ....

    (ii) ....are obtained from stalks by threshing.

    (iii) Husk from wheat flour is generally removed by ....

    (iv) The process of settling of heavier particles is called ....

    (v) Filtration is helpful in separating an insoluble ....
from a ....

Ans. (i) hand-picking

    (ii) Grains (seeds)

    (iii) sieving

    (iv) sedimentation

    (v) solute (solid), solution (liquid)

Q. 13 State whether the following statements are true or false.

    (a) A mixture of oil and water can be separated by filtration.

    (b) Water can be separated from salt by evaporation.

    (c) A mixture of wheat grains and wheat flour can be separated by sieving.

    (d) A mixture of iron filings and rice flour can be separated by magnet.

    (e) A mixture of wheat grains and rice flakes can be separated by winnowing.

    (f) A mixture of tea leaves and milk can be separated by decantation.

Ans. (a) False, A mixture of oil and water can be separated by decantation.

    (b) True   (c) True

    (d) True   (e) True

    (f) True

Short Answer Type Questions

Q. 14 Name and describe briefly a method which can be helpful in separating a mixture of husk from grains. What is the principle of this method?

Ans. Winnowing is used to separate lighter husk particles from heavier seeds of grains by wind or by blowing air.

This method is based on the fact that husk is very light whereas wheat grains are comparatively heavy. The mixture is allowed to fall from a height by shaking winnowing basket continuously. The husk particles are carried away by the wind to a greater distance. The wheat grains, being heavy, fall down vertically to the ground and form a heap of wheat grains.

Q. 15 Match the mixtures in Column I with their methods of separation in Column II.

	Column I		Column II
(a)	Oil mixed in water	(i)	Sieving
(b)	Iron powder mixed with flour	(ii)	Hand-picking
(c)	Salt mixed with water	(iii)	Decantation
(d)	Lady's finger mixed with french beans	(iv)	Magnet
(e)	Rice flour mixed with kidney beans	(v)	Evaporation

Ans. *(c)* The correct matching is as given:
(a)—(iii), (b)—(iv), (c)—(v), (d)—(ii), (e)—(i)

Long Answer Type Questions

Q. 16 Both Sarika and Mohan were asked to make salt solution. Sarika was given a teaspoonful of salt and half a glass of water whereas, Mohan was given twenty teaspoonful of salt and half a glass of water.

(a) How would they make salt solutions?

(b) Who would be able to prepare saturated solution?

Ans. (a) They will mix salt with water within a certain amount to make salt solution. Hence, Sarika will make a better salt solution.

(b) Saturation is the point at which a solution of a substance can dissolve no more of that substance and additional amount of that substance will appear as a precipitate.
Mohan's solution would be saturated because in Mohan's case, some salt would remain undissolved and settled at the bottom of the glass.

Q. 17 Paheli was feeling thirsty but there was only a pot of water at home which was muddy and unfit for drinking. How do you think Paheli would have made this water fit for drinking if the following materials were available to her?
Alum, tub, muslin cloth, gas stove, thread, pan and lid.

Ans. Paheli can make this water fit for drinking by working on following sequence:

Filtration using muslin cloth (cotton fabric).
↓

Swirl with alum (tied with a thread) and leave water undisturbed for some time.
↓

The clear liquid above the impurities is poured in another container (tub) (decantation).
↓

Boil for 10 min on gas stove in covered pan with lid.
↓

Cool, filter and now, it is fit for drinking.

Q. 18 Read the story titled 'Wise Farmer' and tick the correct option to complete the story.

A farmer was sad/happy to see his healthy wheat crops ready for harvest. He harvested the crops and left it under the sun/rain to dry the stalks. To separate the seeds from the bundles of the stalk, he handpicked/threshed them.

After gathering the seed grains, he wanted to separate the stones and husk from it. His wife winnowed/ threshed them to separate the husk and later sieved/ hand-picked to remove stones from it. She ground the wheat grains and sieved/filtered the flour. The wise farmer and his wife got a good price for the flour. Can you tell why?

Ans.   (i) happy   (ii) sun

       (iii) threshed   (iv) winnowed

       (v) hand-picked   (vi) sieved

They got a good price as they used appropriate methods of separation to get good quality of flour (atta).

Q. 19 You are provided with a mixture of salt, sand, oil and water. Write the steps involved for the separation of salt, sand and oil from the mixture by giving an activity along with the diagram.

Ans. **Steps for the separation of salt, sand, oil and water**

First we will use decantation method to separate oil and water. Water being heavier, forms the lower layer and oil being lighter, forms the upper layer in the beaker. We can decant off the upper layer of oil into another beaker carefully.

Then by the process of filtration sand can be separated from water. The filtrate obtained contains the mixture of salt and water. The salt dissolved in water can be separated by the process of evaporation.

The water present in salt solution will form water vapour and then the salt is left behind.

(a) **Decantation**

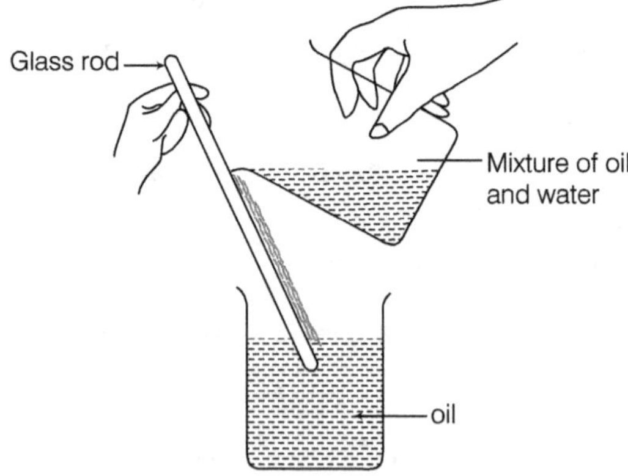

(b) **Filtration**

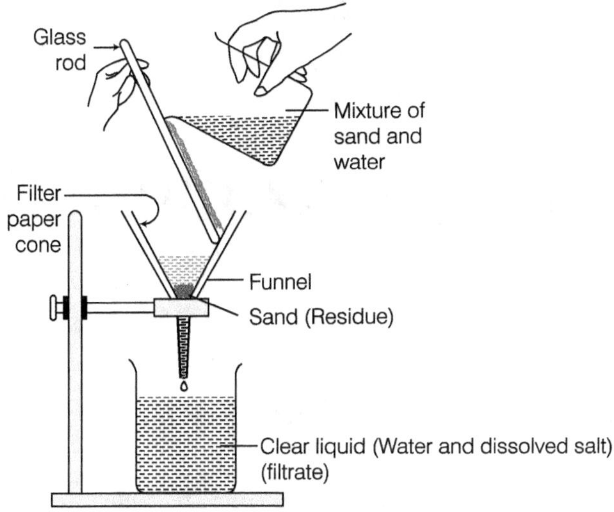

(c) **Evaporation**

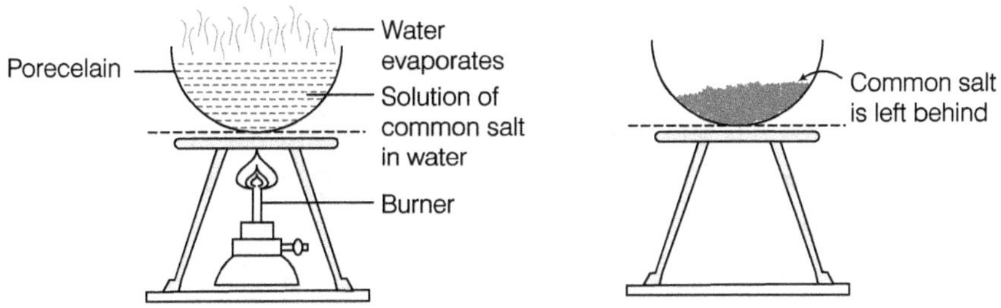

Q. 20 A mixture or iron nails, salt, oil and water is provided to you. Give stepwise method to separate each component from this mixture?

Ans. Steps for the separation of iron nails, salt, oil and water

Iron nails are separated from the mixture by using magnets. Then by using decantation oil and water is separated. Oil being lighter forms the upper layer in the beaker and we can decant off the upper layer of oil.

Now, the mixture contains dissolved salt and water. Salt can be obtained from the water by the process of evaporation. The water present in salt solution will form water vapour and then the salt is left behind.

6

Changes Around US

Multiple Choice Questions (MCQs)

Q. 1 Pick the change that can be reversed from the following.

    (a) Cutting of trees   (b) Melting of ghee

    (c) Burning of candle   (d) Blooming of flower

Ans. *(b)*   Melting of ghee is a reversible change because on melting, ghee turns into liquid form and after cooling it returns back to its original form.

Q. 2 Which of the following changes cannot be reversed?

    (a) Hardening of cement   (b) Freezing of ice cream

    (c) Opening a door   (d) Melting of chocolate

Ans. *(a)*   Hardening of cement is an irreversible change. Changes that cannot be reversed are called irreversible changes.

Q. 3 An iron ring is heated. Which of the following statement about it is incorrect?

    (a) The ring expands

    (b) The ring almost comes to the same size on cooling

    (c) The change in this case is reversed

    (d) The ring changes its shape and the change cannot be reversed

Ans. *(d)*   The correct statement is that when an iron ring is heated the ring expands and the change can be reversed.

Q. 4 While lighting a candle, Paheli observed the following changes:

    (i) Wax was melting.   (ii) Candle was burning.

   (iii) Size of the candle was reducing.

   (iv) Melted wax was getting solidified.

Of the above, the changes that can be reversed are

    (a) (i) and (ii)   (b) (ii) and (iii)   (c) (iii) and (iv)   (d) (i) and (iv)

Ans. *(d)* Melting of wax and solidification of melted wax, both can be seen in case of lighting a candle.

Q. 5 Salt can be separated from its solution (salt dissolved in water) because
   (a) mixing of salt in water is a change that can be reversed by heating and melting of salt
   (b) mixing of salt in water is a change that cannot be reversed
   (c) mixing of salt in water is a permanent change
   (d) mixing of salt in water is a change that can be reversed by evaporation

Ans. *(d)* Mixing of salt in water is a change that can be reversed by evaporation.
   The common salt dissolved in water can be separated by the process of evaporation.

Q. 6 Rolling of chapatti and baking of chapatti are the changes that
   (a) can be reversed
   (b) cannot be reversed
   (c) can be reversed and cannot be reversed, respectively
   (d) cannot be reversed and can be reversed, respectively

Ans. *(c)* Rolling of chapatti can be reversed and baking of chapatti cannot be reversed.

Q. 7 Iron rim is made slightly smaller than the wooden wheel. The rim is usually heated before fixing into the wooden wheel because on heating the iron rim
   (a) expands and fits onto the wooden wheel
   (b) contracts and fits onto the wooden wheel
   (c) no change in the size takes place
   (d) expands first, then on cooling contracts and fits onto the wooden wheel

Ans. *(d)* On heating the iron rim, it expands first, then on cooling it contracts and fits onto the wooden wheel.
   Note *Expansion occurs on heating whereas contraction occurs on cooling.*

Very Short Answer Type Questions

Q. 8 Look at the figures given below, which show three situations (a) burning candle (b) an extinguished candle (c) melting wax.

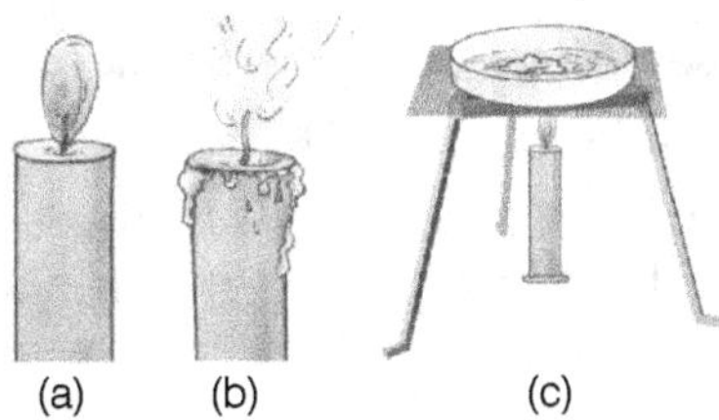

Which of these shows a reversible change and why?

Ans. Melting of wax in (c), which on cooling, changes back to solid wax but burning candle (a) and an extinguished candle (b) show chemical irreversible change.

> **Note** *The burning of wax produces carbon dioxide gas water vapour and soot, which all go into air. We cannot combine all the products of burning of wax to get back the original candle. So burning of candle is an irreversible change.*

Q. 9 A piece of iron is heated till it becomes red hot. It then becomes soft and is beaten to a desired shape. What kind of changes are observed in this process; reversible or irreversible?

Ans. The softening of iron on heating to red hot stage is a reversible change. And when the hot iron is cooled, it becomes hard again.

Q. 10 Paheli had bought a new bottle of pickle from the market. She tried to open the metal cap to taste it but could not do so. She then took a bowl of hot water and immersed the upper end of the bottle in it for five minutes. She could easily open the bottle now. Can you give the reason for this?

Ans. She can easily open the bottle because of expansion of metal cap (increase in size) due to heating.

> **Note** *When a metal object is heated, it increases in size and when the hot object is cooled, it decreases in size and comes back to the original size.*

Short Answer Type Questions

Q. 11 Can we reverse the following changes? If yes, suggest the name of the method.

    (a) Water into water vapour   (b) Water vapour into water

    (c) Ice into water   (d) Curd into milk

Ans. (a) Yes, by **condensation** water vapour can be converted into water.

    (b) Yes, by **evaporation** water converted into its vapour form.

    (c) Yes, by **freezing** water converted into ice.

    (d) Not possible.

Q. 12 Which of the following changes cannot be reversed?

    (a) Blowing of a balloon

    (b) Folding a paper to make a toy aeroplane

    (c) Rolling a ball of dough to make roti

    (d) Baking cake in an oven   (e) Drying a wet cloth

    (f) Making biogas from cow dung   (g) Burning of a candle

Ans. Changes that cannot be reversed are as follows:

    (d) Baking cake in an oven   (f) Making biogas from cow dung

    (g) Burning of a candle

Q. 13 Boojho's sister broke a white dove, a symbol of peace, made of Plaster of Paris (POP). Boojho tried to reconstruct the toy by making a powder of the broken pieces and then making a paste by mixing water. Will he be successful in his effort? Justify your answer.

Ans. Boojho will not be successful because making of toy from Plaster of Paris (POP) is a change that cannot be reversed. Plaster of Paris, immediately sets to a hard mass on adding water to it. So, the setting of plaster of Paris on mixing water is an irreversible chemical change.

Q. 14 Tearing of paper is said to be a change that cannot be reversed. What about paper recycling?

Ans. We can get the paper on paper recycling but it is not the same original paper that we get. The colour and texture of the paper change.

Long Answer Type Questions

Q. 15 Give one example in each case.
    (a) Change which occurs on heating but can be reversed.
    (b) Change which occurs on heating but cannot be reversed.
    (c) Change which occurs on cooling but can be reversed.
    (d) Change which occurs on mixing two substances but can be reversed.
    (e) Change which occurs on mixing two substances but cannot be reversed.

Ans. The example of each case is as follows:
    (a) Heating of an iron rod   (b) Baking of chapatti
    (c) Formation of ice from water   (d) Formation of salt solution
    (e) Mixing of cement and water

Q. 16 A potter working on his wheel shaped a lump of clay into a pot. He then baked the pot in an oven. Do these two acts lead to the same kind of changes or different? Give your opinion and justify your answer.

Ans. These two acts are of different kinds. Making a lump of clay into a pot is a reversible change. This is because the wet clay pot can be converted back into the original clay.

The baking of clay pot in an oven is an irreversible change. This is because the baked clay pot cannot be changed back into the original clay.

Q. 17 Conversion of ice into water and water into ice is an example of change which can be reversed. Give four more examples where you can say that the changes can be reversed.

Ans. Changes that can be reversed are called reversible changes. Some examples are as follows:
    (i) Melting of wax   (ii) Folding of a paper
    (iii) Knitting of a sweater   (iv) Inflating of a tyre

Q. 18 Change of a bud into a flower is a change which cannot be reversed. Give four more such example.

Ans. Changes that cannot be reversed are called irreversible changes. Some examples are as follows :

   (i) Milk into curd   (ii) Burning of wood

   (iii) Ripening of fruits   (iv) Digestion of food

Q. 19 Paheli mixed flour and water and (a) made a dough, (b) rolled the dough to make a chapatti, (c) baked the chapatti on a pan, (d) dried the chapatti and ground it in a grinder to make powder. Identify the changes (a) to (d) as the changes that can be reversed or that cannot be reversed.

Ans. (a) Made a dough this change cannot be reversed.

   (b) Rolled the dough to make a chapatti. This change can be reversed.

   (c) Baked the chapatti on a pan, this change cannot be reversed.

   (d) Dried the chapatti and ground it in a grinder to make powder, this change cannot be reversed.

Q. 20 It was Paheli's birthday, her brother Simba was helping her to decorate the house for the birthday party and their parents were also busy making other arrangements. Following were the activities going on at Paheli's home:

   (a) Simba blew balloons and put them on the wall.

   (b) Some of the balloons got burst.

   (c) Paheli cut colourful strips of paper and put them on the wall with the help of tape.

   (d) She also made some flowers by origami (paper folding) to decorate the house.

   (e) Her father made dough balls.

   (f) Mother rolled the dough balls to make puries.

   (g) Mother heated oil in a pan.

   (h) Father fried the puries in hot oil.

Identify the activities at Paheli's home, as those that can be reversed and those, which cannot be reversed.

Ans. Reversed changes are as follows:

   (a) Simba blew balloons and put them on the wall.

   (d) Making of some flowers by origami (paper folding) to decorate the house.

   (e) Her father made dough balls.

   (f) Mother rolled the dough balls to make puries

   (g) Mother heated oil in a pan.

Changes that cannot be reversed are as follows:

   (b) Some of the balloons got burst.

   (c) Paheli cut colourful strips of paper and put them on the wall with the help of tape.

   (h) Father fried the puries in hot oil.

7

Getting to Know Plants

Multiple Choice Questions (MCQs)

Q. 1 Which of the following combination of features would you observe in grass?

    (a) Parallel venation and fibrous root
    (b) Parallel venation and tap root
    (c) Reticulate venation and fibrous root
    (d) Reticulate venation and tap root

Ans. *(a)* Grass has parallel venation in leaves (veins run parallel to one another on both sides of the mid rib) and fibrous root system (bunch of similar size fibre-like roots).

Q. 2 Which of the following is the correct match between the characteristics of stem and the category of plant?

    (a) Weak stem which cannot stand upright: Creeper
    (b) Green tender stem: Shrub
    (c) Thick, hard stem with branching near the base : Tree
    (d) Thick, hard stem with branches high on the plant : Herb

Ans. *(a)* A **creeper** is a plant having thin, long and weak stem, which cannot stand upright and spreads on the ground, e.g. Money plant. The rest can be corrected as :

Shrub Hard woody stem with branching near the base, e.g. Jasmine.

Tree Hard thick woody stem with branching much above the ground on the stem, e.g. Banyan, neem

Herb Non-woody, soft delicate, green tender stem e.g. Sunflower, tomato.

Q. 3 Which of the following is not the primary function of stem?

    (a) Conduction of water   (b) Photosynthesis
    (c) Formation of branches   (d) Bears flowers and fruits

Ans. *(b)* Photosynthesis is not the primary function of stem. It is a function of leaves. Whereas, conduction of water and minerals from roots to other parts, formation of branches, bearing flowers and fruits and holding the plant upright are main functions of a stem.

Q. 4 Which of the following is not a correct match?

    (a) Petiole: attaches leaf to stem
    (b) Lamina: green flat part of leaf
    (c) Margin: gives shape to the leaf
    (d) Veins: transpiration

Ans. *(d)* Veins provide support to the leaf and carry water and dissolved minerals to the leaf and food away from the leaf. Transpiration takes place through the minute pores on the surface of a leaf called, stomata (transpiration is evaporation of water from plants).

Q. 5 Read the following sentences about photosynthesis.

    (i) Sunlight, carbon dioxide, chlorophyll and water are necessary.
    (ii) Oxygen is absorbed.
    (iii) Leaves carry out photosynthesis.
    (iv) Proteins are made during photosynthesis.

Choose the correct pair of sentences that is true to photosynthesis.

    (a) (iii) and (iv)   (b) (i) and (iii)   (c) (ii) and (iv)   (d) (i) and (iv)

Ans. *(b)* Statements (i) and (iii) are correct.
Photosynthesis is the process by which leaves prepare food. Sunlight, carbon dioxide, chlorophyll and water are necessary for it.
The other sentences can be corrected as:

    (i) Oxygen is released (not absorbed) during this process.
    (ii) Carbohydrates (not proteins) are made during photosynthesis.

Q. 6 Which of the following terms constitute the female part of the flower?

    (a) Sepals, petal and stamen   (b) Stigma, style and ovary
    (c) Ovary, stamen and stigma   (d) Ovary, style and stamen

Ans. *(b)* The **pistil** or **carpel** is the female part of a flower. It is made up of three parts as:
Stigma Top part of pistil. It is sticky and receives pollen.
Style Middle part of pistil. It is a tube that connects stigma to ovary.
Ovary Swollen part at the bottom of pistil that contains ovules.

Very Short Answer Type Questions

Q. 7   (i) The small green leaves at the base of flowers are known as ....
    (ii) The swollen basal part of the pistil is the .... which bears the ....
    (iii) Stamen has two parts called .... and ....
    (iv) The young unopened flower is termed as ....

Ans.   (i) sepals   (ii) ovary; ovules
    (iii) anther; filament   (iv) bud

Q. 8 Solve the riddles given below

    (a) 'I have a green tender stem and I am much shorter than you. Who am I?'

    (b) I come out first from the seed when it is soaked in water. I provide anchorage to plants. Who am I? Write another function that I perform.

Ans. (a) **Herb**, because it has a green tender stem that bends easily and is short-sized (usually do not grow more than 1 m in height).

    (b) **Root** is the first part that comes out of a seed and provides anchorage to plant. Another function that it performs is absorption of water and minerals from the soil.

Short Answer Type Questions

Q. 9 Match the parts of plant given in Column I with their function in Column II.

	Column I		Column II
(a)	Flower	(i)	Excretion
(b)	Leaf	(ii)	Photosynthesis
(c)	Stem	(iii)	Reproduction
(d)	Root	(iv)	Bears branches
		(v)	Anchorage

Ans. The correct matching is as given

(a)—(iii), (b)—(ii), (c)—(iv), (d)—(v)

Note *Plants do not have specialised excretory organs.*

Q. 10 Boojho wanted to test the presence of starch in leaves. He performed the following steps:

    (i) He took a leaf and boiled it in water.

    (ii) He placed the leaf in a petri dish and poured some iodine over it.

He did not get the expected result. Which step did he miss? Explain.

Ans. Boojho did not get the expected results in his experiment because he missed an important step in the procedure.

He did not boil the leaf in alcohol or spirit to remove chlorophyll (green colour) from the leaf. It is necessary to remove chlorophyll because it interferes with the test for starch. The decolourised leaf, on adding iodine turns blue-black, showing the presence of starch.

Q. 11 Will a leaf taken from a potted plant kept in a dark room for a few days turn blue-black when tested for starch? Give reason for your answer.

Ans. No, a leaf from a potted plant kept in dark will not turn blue-black when tested for the presence of starch.

This is because all the stored starch would have been used up by the plant. No fresh starch would be synthesised by leaves due to non-availability of sunlight (i.e. no photosynthesis can occur, thus no food is prepared).

Q. 12 Can the stem of a plant be compared with a street with two ways traffic? Give reason.

Ans. Yes, the stem of a plant can be compared with a street with two ways traffic because movement of substances occur in different directions in it.

(i) It carries water and minerals from the roots to the leaves and other parts of plant in **upward** direction.

(ii) It takes the food prepared by the leaves to other parts of the plant, in **downward** direction.

Long Answer Type Questions

Q. 13 Read the function of parts of a plant given below:

(a) fixes plant to the soil

(b) prepares starch

(c) takes part in reproduction

(d) supports branches and bears flowers

In the diagram, write the names of the parts whose function you have just read at the appropriate space.

Ans. Functions of parts of a plant labelled are :

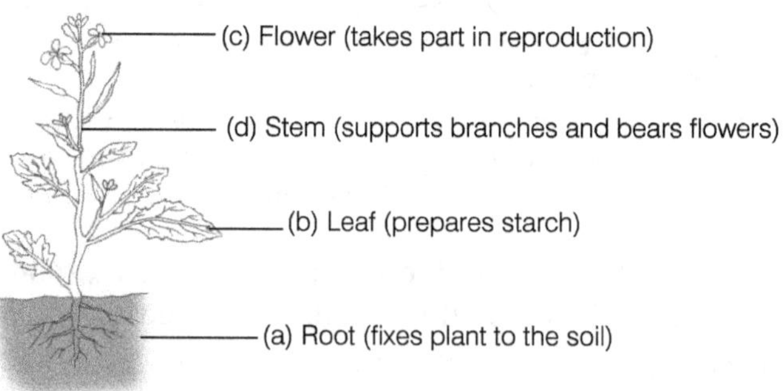

Q. 14 Draw the veins of leaves given in the figure below and write the type of venation.

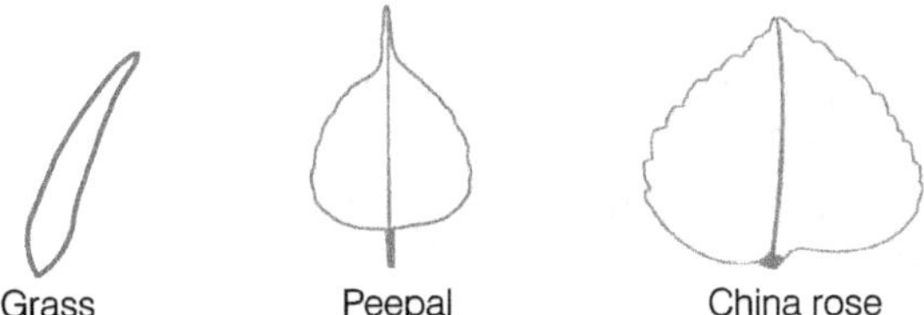

Ans. The veins of leaves and their type of venation are:

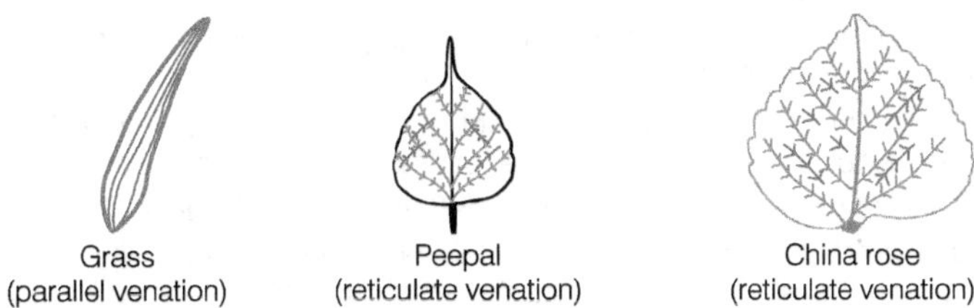

Q. 15 Observe the figure and attempt the questions that follow it.

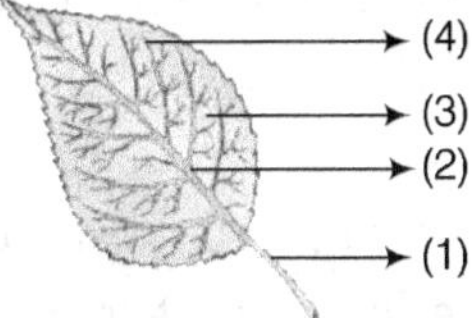

    (a) Label the parts (i), (ii), (iii) and (iv) in the figure.

    (b) What type of venation does the leaf has?

    (c) What type of venation is seen in grass leaves?

Ans. (a) In the given figure:

    (i) Petiole   (ii) Mid rib

    (iii) Lamina   (iv) Vein

    (b) The leaf has reticulate venation, the veins in leaf occur in an irregular way forming a net-like structure.

    (c) Grass leaves have parallel venation. The vein run parallel to each other on both sides of mid rib.

Q. 16 Observe the figure of an activity given as figure, carried out with leaves of plants and polythene bag. Now answer the following.

(a) Which process is demonstrated in the activity?

(b) When will this activity show better results on a bright sunny day or a cloudy day?

(c) What will you observe in the polythene bag after a few hours of setting up the activity?

(d) Mention any one precaution you must take, while performing this activity.

Ans. (a) The process demonstrated in the activity is **transpiration**. It is loss of water in the form of vapour from plant.

(b) The activity will show better results on a bright sunny day because transpiration is maximum in sunlight.

(c) After a few hours of setting up the activity, one can observe small droplets of water inside the polythene bag. Since, the leaves are enclosed in polythene bag, the water vapour cannot escape into air and keeps on collecting inside the polythene bag.

(d) A major precaution one must take, while performing this activity is that the polythene bag should be clean and dry and its mouth should be sealed properly to make the set-up air-tight. Also, the twig should be fresh with 10-12 leaves.

Q. 17 Identify the wrong statements and correct them.

(a) Anther is a part of the pistil.

(b) The visible parts of a bud are the petals.

(c) Lateral roots are present in a tap root.

(d) Leaves perform the function of transpiration only.

Ans. (a) It is wrong.

Correct statement - Anther is a part of **stamen**.

(b) It is wrong.

Correct statement - Visible part of a bud are the **sepals**.

(c) It is correct.

Tap root is the main root and the smaller side roots are called lateral roots.

(d) It is wrong.

Correct statement - Leaves perform three main functions, i.e. photosynthesis, transpiration and respiration.

Q. 18 Solve the crossword given in figure as per the clues given below it.

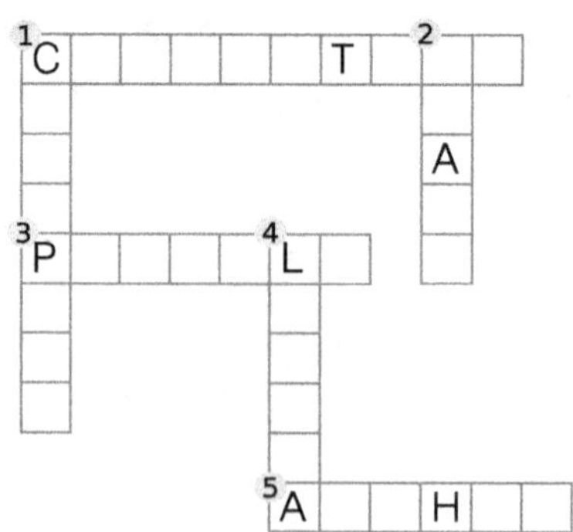

Across

1. The term that describes upward movement of water in a stem.
3. The part of leaf, which is attached to the stem.
5. This part is attached to the tip of filament.

Down

1. Plants that are weak and spread on the ground.
2. Ovules are present in this part of flower.
4. It is the broad part of leaf.

Ans. **Across**

1. CONDUCTION   3. PETIOLE
5. ANTHER

Down

1. CREEPERS   2. OVARY
4. LAMINA

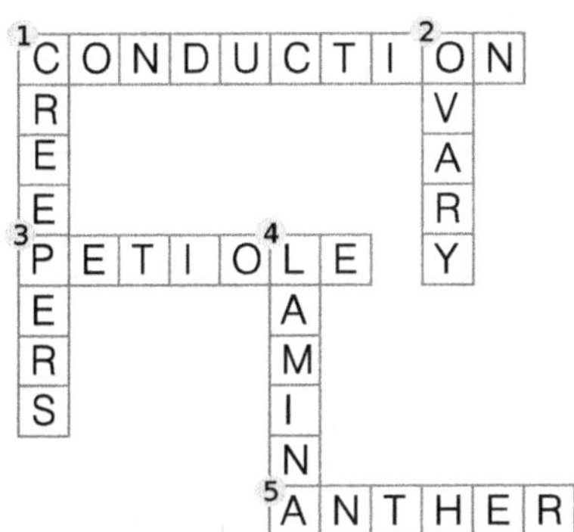

Q. 19 Fill in the blanks with the terms that are listed below. [anther, male, ovary, ovule, petals, pistil, stamen, filament]. Sepals ...(a)..., stamens and ...(b)... are the parts of a flower. Stamen is made up of ...(c)... and ...(d)... and it represents the ...(e)... part of the flower. The female part of the flower is called the ...(f).... The basal, swollen part of the pistil is called the ...(g)... which contains the ...(h)..... .

Ans.   (a) petals   (b) pistil
         (c) anther   (d) filament
         (e) male   (f) pistil
         (g) ovary   (h) ovules

8

Body Movement

Multiple Choice Questions (MCQs)

Q. 1 Which of the following parts of our body help us in movement?

    (i) Bones   (ii) Skin

    (iii) Muscles   (iv) Organs

Choose the correct answer from the option below.

    (a) (i) and (iii)   (b) (ii) and (iv)

    (c) (i) and (iv)   (d) (ii) and (iii)

Ans. *(a)* Our bones and muscles together form the musculoskeletal system that enables the movement of body parts and the whole body from one place to another.

Q. 2 Which of the following joints are immovable?

    (a) Shoulder and arm   (b) Knee and joint

    (c) Upper jaw and skull   (d) Lower jaw and upper jaw

Ans. *(c)* Upper jaw and skull joints are immovable or fixed. Bones are held, so tightly together that they cannot move at all. The other options are:

Shoulder and arm Ball and socket joint

Knee and joint Hinge joint

Lower jaw and upper jaw Hinge joint

Q. 3 Which of the following organisms does not have both muscles and skeleton for movement?

    (a) Dog   (b) Snail

    (c) Earthworm   (d) Human being

Ans. *(b)* Snail does not have both muscles and skeleton for movement. The shell (i.e. external skeleton) serves for muscles attachment and protection. The movement is carried out only with the help of large disc-shaped muscular foot that has two sets of muscles.

In earthworm, a hydrostatic skeleton (fluid filled cavity surrounded by muscles) is present. The alternate contraction and relaxation of muscles and pressure of the fluid helps in burrowing.

Dog and human beings have musculoskeletal system for movement.

Q. 4 Underwater divers wear fin-like flippers on their feet to

    (a) swim easily in water
    (b) look like a fish
    (c) walk on water surface
    (d) walk over the bottom of the sea (sea bed)

Ans. *(a)* The fin-like flippers worn by underwater divers help to swim easily in water. It mainly helps to keep the balance of the body and to keep direction, while swimming (just as fins in fishes).

Q. 5 Snail moves with the help of its

    (a) shell   (b) bone
    (c) muscular foot   (d) whole body

Ans. *(c)* Snail moves with the help of a large, disc-shaped muscular foot.
The whole body of a snail is soft and consists of a head, a foot and a shell. Shell is the outer structure (skeleton) of snail, but it is not made of bones.

Q. 6 How many muscles work together to move a bone?

    (a) One   (b) Two
    (c) Three   (d) Four

Ans. *(b)* Two muscles (a pair) work together to move a bone. When one muscle of the pair contracts, then the other muscle of the pair is relaxed. The alternate contraction and stretching brings about the movement.

Very Short Answer Type Questions

Q. 7 Name the type of joints of your hand which helps you to grasp a badminton racquet.

Ans. Hinge joint of our hand helps us to grasp a badminton racquet.

Q. 8 What would have happened, if our backbone was made up of one single bone?

Ans. If our backbone was made up of one single bone, then we would not have been able to bend our body (from waist). Therefore, it is made up of 33 small bones called vertebrae.

Q. 9 Provide one word answer to the statements given below.

    (a) Joint which allows movement in all directions.
    (b) Hard structure that forms the skeleton.
    (c) Part of the body with a fixed joint.
    (d) Help in the movement of body by contraction and relaxation.

(e) Bones that join with chest bone at one end and to the backbone at the other end.

(f) Framework of bones which gives shape to our body.

(g) Bones which enclose the organs of our body that lie below the abdomen.

(h) Joint where our neck joins the head.

(i) Part of the skeleton that forms the earlobe.

Ans.

(a) Ball and socket joint

(b) Bones

(c) Upper jaw with skull

(d) Muscles

(e) Rib

(f) Skeleton

(g) Pelvic bones

(h) Pivotal

(i) Cartilage

Q. 10 Write the type of joint which is used for each of the following movements:

(a) A cricket bowler bowls the ball.

(b) A girls move her head in right and left direction.

(c) A person lifts weights to build up his biceps.

Ans.

(a) It involves the shoulder joint, i.e. Ball and socket joint.

(b) It involves pivot joint that connects our head to the neck.

(c) It involves the elbow joint i.e. Hinge joint.

Short Answer Type Questions

Q. 11 Match the name of the animals given in Column I with its body parts used for movement given in Column II.

	Column I		Column II
(a)	Human being	(i)	Fins
(b)	Cow	(ii)	Wings
(c)	Snake	(iii)	Legs
(d)	Eagle	(iv)	Whole body
(e)	Fish	(v)	Limbs

Ans. The correct matching is as given:

(a)—(iii), (b)—(v), (c)—(iv), (d)—(ii), (e)—(i)

Q. 12 Given below is a list of different types of movements in animals:
Running, jumping, walking, slithering, crawling, flying, swimming, creeping.

Write the types of movements seen in each animal.

(a) Duck	(b) Horse
(c) Kangaroo	(d) Snail
(e) Snake	(f) Fish
(g) Human being	(h) Cockroach

Ans. The types of movements seen in each animals are as follows:

(a) Duck	— Flying, walking and swimming
(b) Horse	— Running and walking
(c) Kangaroo	— Jumping and walking
(d) Snail	— Creeping
(e) Snake	— Slithering
(f) Fish	— Swimming
(g) Human being	— Walking and running
(h) Cockroach	— Walking and flying (short distances)

Q. 13 Bhoojho fell off a tree and hurt his ankle. On examination, the doctor confirmed that the ankle was fractured. How was it detected?

Ans. The doctor must have observed a swelling around his ankle and taken an X-ray of his ankle. X-ray images confirm any type of injuries/fractures in the bones.

Q. 14 Bones are hard structures and cannot be bent. But, we can still bend our elbow, knee, etc. How is this possible?

Ans. Elbow and knee are not made up of a single bone rather they are made up of two or more bones which are joined to each other by a joint, i.e. hinge joint. This joint along with the muscles help us to bend the elbow and knee. Hinge joint allows the movement of bones in only one direction.

Q. 15 Which type of movement would have been possible if

(a) our elbow had a fixed joint.

(b) we were to have a ball and socket joint between our neck and head.

Ans. (a) If our elbow had a fixed joint, we would not be able to bend/fold our arms. A fixed joint does not allow any movement.

(b) If we were to have a ball and socket joint between our neck and head, we would be able to rotate our head 360°. A ball and socket joint allows movement in all directions.

Q. 16 Earthworms are known as farmer's friends. Why?

Ans. Earthworms make their way through the soil, by loosening the soil and allowing more air to get in. Their body excretes undigested materials that also increases the fertility of soil.

They also help in the decomposition of organic wastes and stabilise a wide variety of wastes. This is called vermicomposting. All this helps the crops to grow, that is why earthworms are regarded as farmer's friends.

Long Answer Type Questions

Q. 17 (a) Unscramble the jumbled words and write them in the blank spaces provided.

   (i) neosb ....   (ii) tnemevom ....

  (iii) iontcaronct ....   (iv) lsecsum ....

   (v) arctigeal ....   (vi) epahs ....

 (vii) sangro inerlant ....   (viii) laxaeriont ....

  (b) Read the following paragraph and fill in the blanks using the words you unscrambled.

    ...(i)... and ...(ii)... form the skeleton of the human body. They provide the framework, give ...(iii)... to the body and help in ...(iv)... . They protect the ...(v)... . The bones are moved by alternate ...(vi)... and ...(vii)... of two sets of ...(viii)... attached to them.

Ans. (a) (i) bones (ii) movement (iii) contraction (iv) muscles (v) cartilage (vi) shape (vii) internal organs (viii) relaxation

  (b) (i) **Bones** and (ii) **cartilage** form the skeleton of the human body. They provide the framework, give (iii) **shape** to the body and help in (iv) **movement**. They protect the (v) **internal organs**. The bones are moved by alternate (vi) **contraction** and (vii) **relaxation** of two sets of (viii) **muscles** attached to them.

Q. 18 How is the skeleton of a bird well-suited for flying?

Ans. The skeleton of a bird is well-suited for flying because

  (i) Their bones are hollow and light in weight.

  (ii) Their forelimbs are modified as wings.

  (iii) The shoulder bones are strong, thus helpful in flying.

  (iv) The breast bones are modified to hold flight muscles which are used to move the wings up and down for flying.

  (v) They have a streamlined body, which reduces the air resistance.

Q. 19 In the figure given below, there are two snakes of the same size slithering on sand. Can you identify which of them would move faster and why?

Ans. Snakes do not have limbs but have rough scales on the underside of the body that help them in their locomotion. A snake form loops in its body while slithering. Each loop of the snake gives it a forward push by pressing against the ground. The snake with a larger number of loops will move much faster than the snake with lesser number of loops.

Thus, snake *A* will move faster than snake *B* as we can see more loops are formed by snake *A*.

9

The Living Organisms and Their Surroundings

Multiple Choice Questions (MCQs)

Q. 1 Which of the following cannot be called a habitat?

    (a) A desert with camels   (b) A pond with fishes

    (c) A jungle with wild animals   (d) Cultivated land with grazing cattle

Ans. *(d)* Cultivated land with grazing cattle cannot be called a habitat. The cattle does not live in the cultivated land. They come there, only for feeding. A habitat is the surroundings where organisms live. It means a dwelling place, e.g. aquatic habitats such as pond.

Q. 2 Following are some features of plants.

    (i) They lose a lot of water through transpiration.

    (ii) Their leaves are always broad and flat.

    (iii) They lose very little water through transpiration.

    (iv) Their roots grow very deep into the soil.

Which of the combination of given features are typical of desert plants?

    (a) (i) and (ii)   (b) (ii) and (iv)

    (c) (ii) and (iii)   (d) (iii) and (iv)

Ans. *(d)* Features of desert plants that help them to survive there are:
- Lose very little water through transpiration.
- Leaves are either absert, very small or reduced to spines.
- Stem is covered with thick waxy layer to retain water.
- Root grow very deep into the soil for absorbing water.

Q. 3 Boojho comes across an animal having a stream-lined and slippery body. What is the habitat of the animal?

    (a) Water   (b) Desert

    (c) Grassland   (d) Mountain

Ans. (*a*) The animal having a stream-lined and slippery body lives in water habitat. These are adaptations to survive in water.
Stream-lined bodies reduce resistance due to water and help in swimming.
The slippery body makes movement through water easier.
The other adaptations of these animals are gills for breathing, flat fins, tails, etc.

Q. 4 Which of the following are characteristics of living beings?

(i) Respiration
(ii) Reproduction
(iii) Adaptation
(iv) Excretion

Choose the correct answer from the options below.

(a) (i), (ii) and (iv)   (b) (i) and (ii)
(c) (ii) and (iv)   (d) (i), (ii), (iii) and (iv)

Ans. (*d*) The living beings have some common characteristic that makes them different from the non-living. These are respiration, reproduction, adaptations, excretion, growth, nutrition and movement.

Q. 5 Earthworms breathe through their

(a) skin   (b) gills
(c) lungs   (d) stomata

Ans. (*a*) Earthworms breathe through their skin. Their skin is thin and moist with plenty of blood supply for exchange of gases.
The other options are used by other organisms such as gills–fishes, lungs–humans and stomata–plants.

Q. 6 Which of the following is not an example of response to stimulus?

(a) Watering in mouth when we see delicious food items
(b) Closing of leaves of *Mimosa* plant when touched
(c) Shutting our eyes when an object is suddenly thrown in our direction
(d) A chick hatching out of an egg

Ans. (*d*) A chick hatching out of an egg is not a response to stimuli, it is a natural phenomenon of reproduction in hens that requires particular time period and temperature to occur.
The other options are examples of response to changes in our surroundings (stimuli) which is a characteristic of living beings.

Q. 7 Which of the following is correct for respiration in plants?

(a) Respiration takes place only during day time
(b) Respiration takes place only during night
(c) Respiration takes place both during day and night
(d) Respiration takes place only when plants are not making food

Ans. (*c*) In plants, respiration, takes place both during day and night. During daytime, all the CO_2 produced in respiration is used up by plants for photosynthesis and only oxygen produced during photosynthesis is released. The plants give out CO_2 produced in respiration only at night time.

Q. 8 Which of the following is an incorrect statement about excretion?

    (a) Excretion takes place in plants.

    (b) Excretion takes place both in plants and animals.

    (c) Excretion is the process of getting rid of excess water only.

    (d) Secretion is one method of excretion.

Ans. *(c)* Excretion is the process of removal of waste substances from the body of a living organism. The wastes include not just excess water but CO_2, nitrogenous matter, feaces, etc.

It is an important characteristic of living organisms.

Q. 9 Choose the set that represents only the biotic components of a habitat.

    (a) Tiger, deer, grass, soil   (b) Rocks, soil, plants, air

    (c) Sand, turtle, crab, rocks   (d) Aquatic plant, fish, frog, insect

Ans. *(d)* Aquatic plant, fish, frog, insect represents only the biotic components of a habitat. The living things such as plants, animals and microorganisms in a habitat are known as its biotic components.

Soil (in a), rocks, soil and air (in b) and sand and rocks (in c) are the abiotic (non-living) components.

Q. 10 Which one of the following is not associated with reproduction?

    (a) A new leaf coming out of a tree branch

    (b) A dog giving birth to puppy

    (c) A seed growing into a plant

    (d) Chick hatching from an egg

Ans. *(a)* A new leaf coming out of a tree branch is not associated with reproduction. It is associated with growth.

Reproduction is the process by which living things produce more of their own kind, e.g. dog giving birth to puppy, seed growing into plant and chick hatching from egg.

Q. 11 Choose the odd one out from below with respect to reproduction.

    (a) Eggs of hen   (b) Seeds of plants

    (c) Buds of potato   (d) Roots of mango tree

Ans. *(d)* Roots of mango tree is odd one as its not related to reproduction.

The other options are directly linked to reproduction.

Chickens are hatched from the **eggs of hen**.

Many plants reproduce through **seeds**.

Buds of potato tuber can grow to produce new potato plant.

Q. 12 Although organisms die, their kind continue to live on earth. Which characteristic of living organisms makes this possible?

    (a) Respiration   (b) Reproduction

    (c) Excretion   (d) Movement

Ans. *(b)* Reproduction is the characteristic of living organisms through which they produce more of their own kind.

Thus, even after the organisms die, their kind continue to live on earth.

Short Answer Type Questions

Q. 13 If you happen to go to a desert, what changes do you expect to observe in the urine you excrete? You would

    (i) excrete small amount of urine

    (ii) excrete large amount of urine

    (iii) excrete concentrated urine

    (iv) excrete very dilute urine

Which of the above would hold true?

(a) (i) and (iii)	(b) (ii) and (iv)
(c) (i) and (iv)	(d) (i) and (ii)

Ans. *(a)* A small amount of concentrated urine would be excreted in desert. This will help conserve water in the body.

Q. 14 Unscramble the given words below to get the correct word using the clues given against them.

    (a)   SATPADAOINT   Specific features or certain habits which enable a living being to live in its surroundings.

    (b)   RETECOXNI   Waste products are removed by this process

    (c)   LUMISIT   All living things respond to these

    (d)   ROUCDPRENTOI   Because of this we find organisms of the same kind

Ans.

(a) Adaptations	(b) Excretion
(c) Stimuli	(d) Reproduction

Q. 15 Using the following words, write the habitat of each animal given in figures (a to d).

Grassland, mountain, desert, pond, river

    (a)   (b)   (c)   (d)

Ans.   (a) The diagram is of a deer which lives in grassland.

       (b) The diagram is of a frog which lives in pond.

       (c) The diagram is of a yak which lives in mountain.

       (d) The diagram is of a camel which lives in desert.

Q. 16 Classify the following habitats into terrestrial and aquatic types. Grassland, pond, ocean, rice field

Ans. The habitats can be classified as :

Terrestrial habitats Grassland and rice field. These are land based habitats.

Aquatic habitats Pond and ocean. These are water based habitats.

Q. 17 Why is reproduction important for organisms?

Ans. Reproduction is important for organisms as it leads to the production of more individuals of its own kind. This helps in continuity of life on the earth.

Q. 18 Fill in the blanks:

    (a) Saline water, hot air and sand are .... components of a habitat.

    (b) The habitat of plants and animals that live in .... is called the aquatic habitat.

    (c) .... enable a plant or an animal to live in its surroundings.

    (d) Plants and animals that live on land are said to live in .... habitats.

Ans. (a) Abiotic (non-living)

    (b) Water

    (c) Adaptations

    (d) Terrestrial

Short Answer Type Questions

Q. 19 Paheli has a rose plant in her garden. How can she increase the number of rose plants in the garden?

Ans. Paheli can increase the number of rose plants in the garden by planting stem cutting (a small piece of stem) of the rose plant. The cutting should be made in such a way that there are some buds on it. Its lower part is buried in moist soil.

After a few days, the cuttings develop roots and grow into new plant. Thus, the number of plants increase.

Q. 20 Why do desert snakes burrow deep into the sand during the day?

Ans. Snakes in the desert burrow deep into the sand during the day time when it is very hot because the deeper layers of sand are cooler. This allows them to stay away from heat of the desert that persists through the day time as well as prevent loss of water from their body.

Q. 21 Write the adaptation in aquatic plants due to which

    (a) submerged leaves can bend in the flowing water.

    (b) leaves can float on the surface of water.

Ans. The adaptations are:

    (a) Leaves of aquatic plants are narrow and thin ribbon-like which allow them to bend in the flowing water.

    (b) Stems/Stalks of leaves of aquatic plants are long soft, hollow and light which allow them to float on the surface of water.

Q. 22 Mention one adaptation present in the following animals.

    (a) In camels to keep their bodies away from the heat of sand.

    (b) In frogs to enable them to swim.

    (c) In dolphins and whales to breathe in air when they swim near the surface of water.

Ans. (a) Camels have long legs to keep their bodies away from the heat of sand in desert.

    (b) Frogs have webbed feet that enable them to swim.

    (c) Dolphins and whales have blow holes which help them to breathe in air when they swim near the surface of water.

Q. 23 Some desert plants have very small leaves, whereas some others have only spines. How does this benefit the plants?

Ans. Desert plants have very small leaves or spines as adaptation to dry conditions of the desert. Because of these modifications of leaves, the surface of lamina is reduced which reduces water loss from the leaves through transpiration.

Since very little water is lost through transpiration, that benefits the desert plants to survive on stored food for long time.

Q. 24 What are the specific features present in a deer that help it to detect the presence of predators like lion?

Ans. Deer have following specific features that help it to detect the presence of predators like lion in a forest or grassland:

    (i) Big ears to hear movement of predators very easily.

    (ii) Eyes on the sides of its head which allow it to see in all directions at the same time.

Q. 25 Read the features of plants given below.

    (a) Thick waxy stem

    (b) Short roots

    (c) Cone-shaped plants

    (d) Sloping branches

    (e) Small or spine-like leaves

    (f) Hollow stem

Choose the type of plant for every adaptive feature given in a, b, c, d, e and f from the list given below:

Aquatic plant, desert plant, mountainous plant

Ans. Given below are the features with respect to their corresponding type of plant:
  (a) Thick waxy stem – **desert** plant
  (b) Short roots – **aquatic** plant
  (c) Cone-shaped plants – **mountainous** plant
  (d) Sloping branches – **mountainous** plant
  (e) Small or spine-like leaves – **desert** plant
  (f) Hollow stem – **aquatic** plant

Long Answer Type Questions

Q. 26 Like many animals although a car also moves it is not considered as a living organism. Give two or three reasons.

Ans. A moving car although moves is not considered as a living organism because of the following reasons:
  (i) Living organisms have the ability to move on their own, whereas a car moves by burning of fuels like diesel and petrol.
  (ii) A car does not show any other living characteristics like respiration, digestion, reproduction or growth, that are shown by all living organisms and these processes are essential for living beings.

Q. 27 What are the adaptive features of a lion that helps it in hunting?

Ans. Adaptive features of a lion that helps it in hunting are :
  (i) Long sharp claws in its front legs to catch prey.
  (ii) Eyes placed in front of head allow it to know the correct location and movement of its prey.
  (iii) Brown body colour helps it to hide in dry grassland, this avoids the detection by its prey.

10

Motion and Measurement of Distances

Multiple Choice Questions (MCQs)

Q. 1 The distance between Delhi and Mumbai is usually expressed in units of
  (a) decametre
  (b) metre
  (c) centimetre
  (d) kilometre

Ans. *(d)* The distance between Delhi and Mumbai is expressed in kilometre because other units like metre, centimetre and decametre are so small to express this big distance.

Q. 2 Which of the following does not express a time interval?
  (a) A day
  (b) A second
  (c) A school period
  (d) Time of the first bell in the school

Ans. *(d)* Time of the first bell in the school does not express a time interval because it has only a single value of time, while the other quantities like a day, a second and a school period can be divided into a number of shorter periods of time.

Note *A time interval should have atleast two values of time.*

Q. 3 Figure shows a measuring scale which is usually supplied with a geometry box. Which of the following distance cannot be measured with this scale by using it only once?

  (a) 0.1 m   (b) 0.15 m
  (c) 0.2 m   (d) 0.05 m

Ans. *(c)* Here, $0.1\,m = 10\,cm$

     $0.15\,m = 15\,cm$ $[\because 1\,m = 100\,cm]$

     $0.2\,m = 20\,cm$

and $0.05\,m = 5\,cm$

The distances 10 cm, 15 cm and 5 cm can be easily measured by using a 15 cm long scale, while the distance 20 cm (= 0.2 m) cannot be measured by using this scale only once.

Q. 4 A piece of ribbon folded five times is placed along a 30 cm long measuring scale as shown in figure.

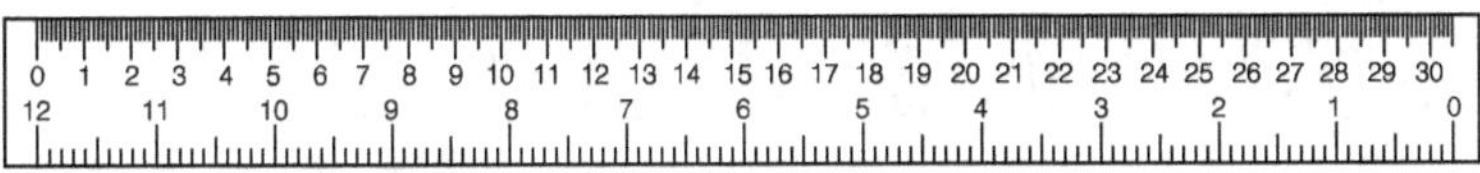

The length of the ribbon is between

(a) 1.15 m-1.25 m

(b) 1.25 m-1.35 m

(c) 1.50 m-1.60 m

(d) 1.60 m-1.70 m

Ans. *(b)* Since, ribbon is folded 5 times, i.e. from figure,

length of ribbon $= (27.5 - 2)\,cm \times 5$

$= (25.5 \times 5)\,cm$

$= 127.5\,cm = 1.27\,m$ $[\because 1\,m = 100\,cm]$

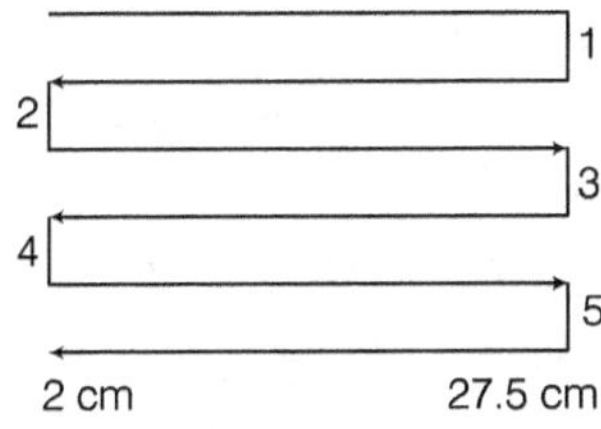

1.27 m lies in the range of 1.25 m – 1.35 m.

Q. 5 Paheli moves on a straight road from point *A* to point *C*. She takes 20 min to cover a certain distance *AB* and 30 min to cover the rest of distance *BC*. She then turns back and takes 30 min to cover the distance *CB* and 20 min to cover the rest of the distance to her starting point. She makes 5 rounds on the road in the same way. Paheli concludes that her motion is

(a) only rectilinear motion

(b) only periodic motion

(c) rectilinear and periodic motion

(d) neither rectilinear nor periodic

Ans. *(c)*   We can understand this using the following diagram:

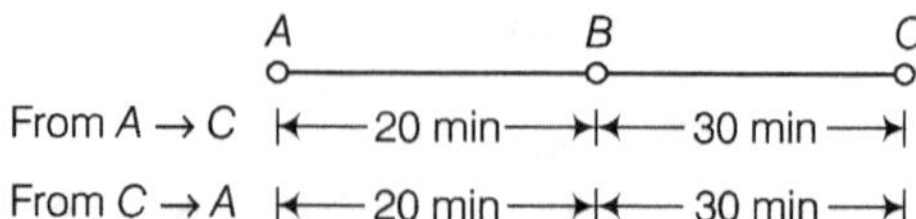

Thus, we can see that Paheli moves in a straight path from $A \to C$ and from $C \to A$. So, the motion is rectilinear, further Paheli moves in a periodic motion because she makes 5 rounds in the same way and crosses point B in each round, after a regular time interval. So, her motion is rectilinear and periodic.

Q. 6 Bholu and Golu are playing on a ground. They start running from the same point A in the ground and reach point B at the same time by following the paths marked 1 and 2, respectively as shown in the figure. Which of the following is true for the given situation?

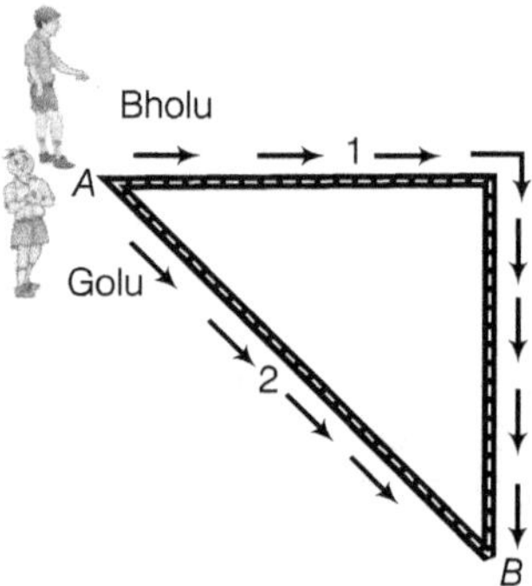

As compared to Golu, Bholu covers a

(a) longer distance but with a lower speed

(b) longer distance with a higher speed

(c) shorter distance with a lower speed

(d) shorter distance with a higher speed

Ans. *(b)*   It is clear from the figure that Bholu covers more distance, since he is on the track which is longer than that of Golu. Both reaches point B at the same time, so Bholu will have to move faster in order to cover more distance (Golu is on the track having the shortest distance between A and B). Therefore, Bholu moves with a higher speed than Golu.

Q. 7 Four pieces of wooden sticks A, B, C and D are placed along the length of 30 cm long scale as shown in figure. Which one of them is 3.4 cm in length?

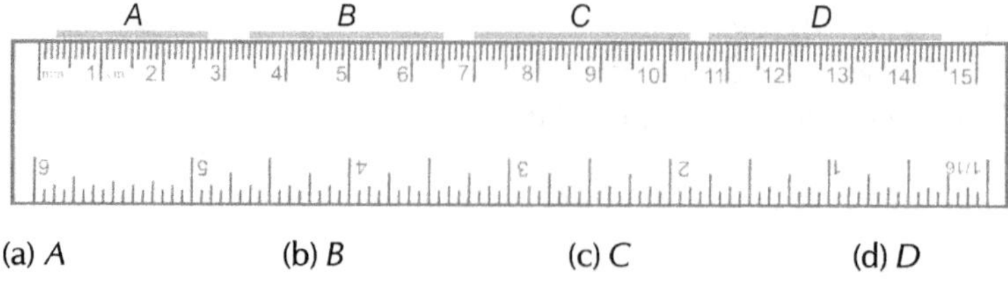

(a) A   (b) B   (c) C   (d) D

Ans. *(c)* From the figure it is clear that,

length of $A = (2.7 - 0.3)\,\text{cm} = 2.4\,\text{cm}$,

length of $B = (6.5 - 3.4)\,\text{cm} = 3.1\,\text{cm}$

length of $C = (10.4 - 7.0)\,\text{cm} = 3.4\,\text{cm}$ and

length of $D = (14.4 - 10.7)\,\text{cm} = 3.7\,\text{cm}$

So, length of C is same as asked, i.e. 3.4 cm.

Q. 8 Which of the following figure shows the correct placement of a block along a scale for measuring its length?

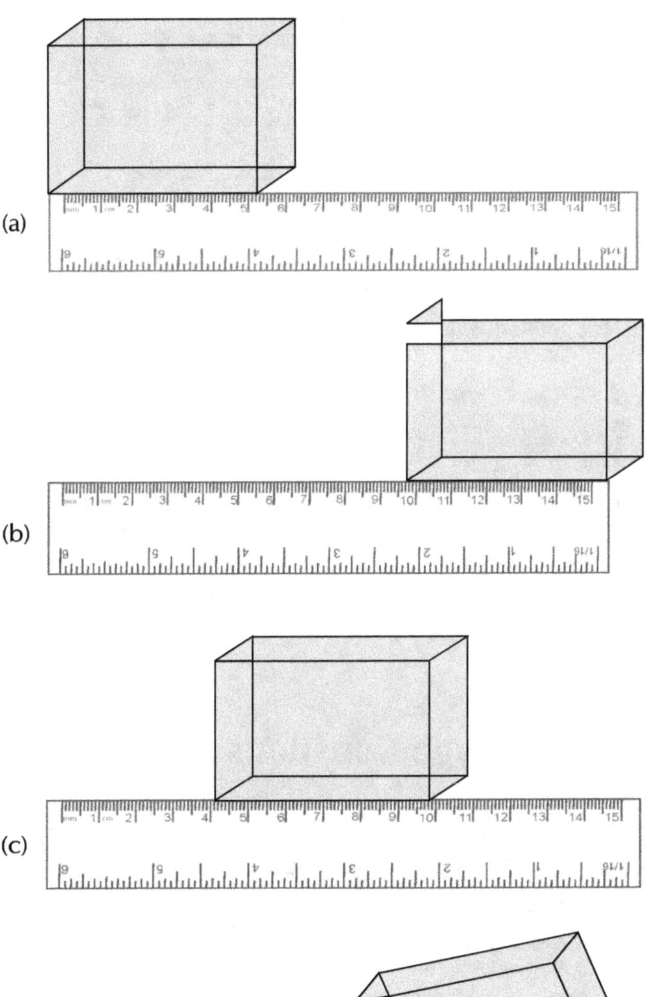

(a)

(b)

(c)

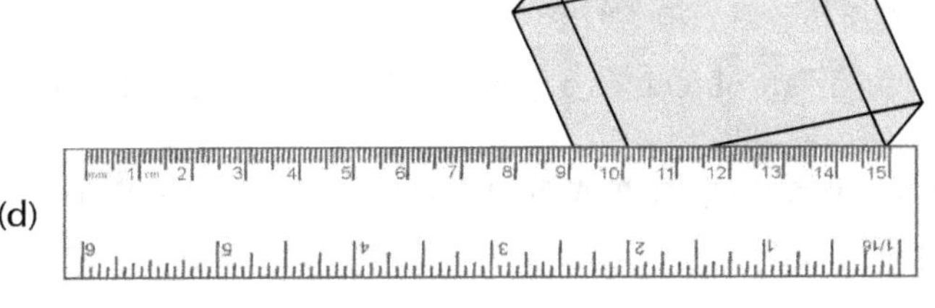

(d)

Ans. *(c)* We can see that (a), (b) and (d) have the placement of block which is going out of the marking of 15 cm scale. Only (c) has the placement which is inside the marking of scale.

Q. 9 You are provided three scales *A, B* and *C* as shown in figure to measure a length of 10 cm.

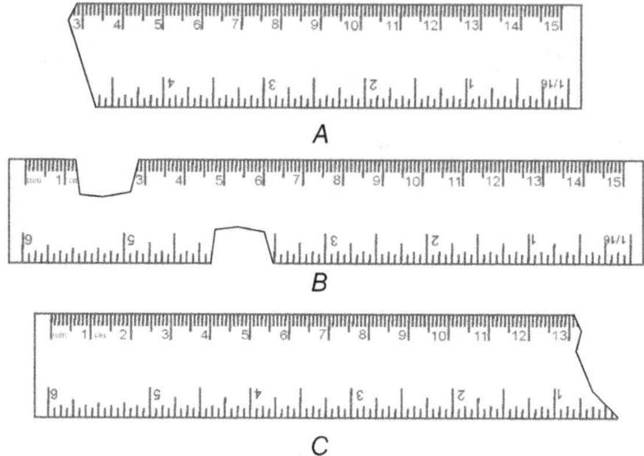

For the correct measurement of the length, you will use the scale
(a) only *A*
(b) only *B*
(c) only *C*
(d) Any of the three scales

Ans. *(d)* We can see that all the scales have 10 cm length interval on their non-broken sides. So, for scale *A*, length of interval available = 15 − 3 = 12 cm

For scale *B*, length of interval available = 15 − 3 = 12 cm

For scale *C*, length of interval available = 13 − 0 = 13 cm

So, (d) is correct option.

Very Short Answer Type Questions

Q. 10 Correct the following.
(a) The motion of a swing is an example of rectilinear motion.
(b) 1 m = 1000 cm

Ans. (a) The motion of a swing is an example of periodic motion. Since, it repeats its motion after a regular interval of time.

(b) 1 m = 100 cm [Each metre (m) has hundred equal divisions, called centimetre (cm)]

Q. 11 (i) Motion of an object or a part of it around a fixed point is known as
.... motion.

(ii) A body repeating its motion after certain interval of time is in .... motion.

    (iii) In rectilinear motion, object moves........... a .... line.

    (iv) The SI unit of length is ....

Ans.   (i) circular

> **Note** *In circular motion an object moves such that its distance from a fixed point remains the same.*

  (ii) periodic, e.g. motion of pendulum of wall clock.

  (iii) along straight, e.g. motion of a vehicle on a straight road.

  (iv) metre

Q. 12 Give one example for each of the following type of motion.

    (a) Rectilinear

    (b) Circular

    (c) Periodic

    (d) Circular and periodic

Ans.   (a) Motion of a stone falling from a height.

  (b) Motion of a point marked on blades of a rotating fan.

  (c) Motion of moon around the earth.

  (d) Motion of hands of a clock.

Short Answer Type Questions

Q. 13 The photograph given in figure shows a section of a grille made up of straight and curved iron bars. How would you measure the length of the bars of this section, so that the payment could be made to the contractor?

Ans. The length of straight iron bars of grille is measured directly with a measuring tape.

For curved iron bars, the length can be measured using a thread which can be further measured with the help of measuring tape.

Q. 14 Identify the different types of motion in the following word diagram given as in the figure.

Y	O	U	N	G	C	C	N	T	E	R
L	E	V	E	L	P	I	E	E	A	R
A	L	L	O	T	O	P	P	E	A	I
N	O	T	N	P	A	D	N	E	C	K
O	W	O	N	E	W	I	Y	Z	S	E
I	E	V	O	R	L	O	A	D	W	P
T	R	G	N	I	C	E	D	R	I	L
A	Z	H	T	O	N	G	U	E	N	A
T	X	C	R	D	E	P	T	H	G	R
O	E	Y	C	I	R	C	U	L	A	R
R	T	L	C	C	O	P	P	E	R	T

Ans. The different types of motion in the following word diagram is as given:

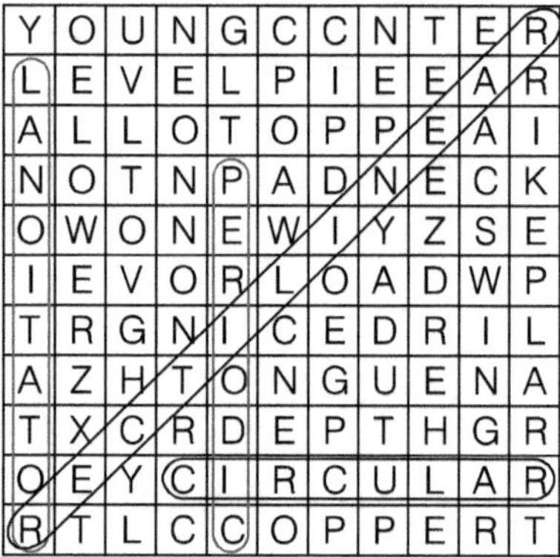

Motion is defined as a change in the position of an object with time. The four types of motion given in the above word diagram are

(i) Rectilinear   (ii) Circular

(iii) Periodic   (iv) Rotational

Q. 15 Four children measure the length of a table which was about 2 m. Each of them used different ways to measure it.

(a) Shyam measured it with a half metre long thread.

(b) Gurmeet measured it with a 15 cm scale from her geometry box.

(c) Reena measured it using her handspan.

(d) Salim measured it using a 5 m long measuring tape.

Which one of them would get the most accurate length? Give reason for your answer.

Ans. (*d*) Salim will measure it most accurately because of the following reasons:

(i) Length 2 m which he wants to measure can be measured using this scale only in a single attempt.

(ii) This scale is standard scale and will give the correct measurement.

Other scales given are either non-standard or having the length less than the length we want to measure.

Q. 16 Match the Column I with Column II.

	Column I		Column II
(a)	A moving wheel of a sewing machine	(i)	Circular motion
(b)	Movement of tip of the minute hand of a clock in one hour	(ii)	Rotational motion
(c)	A moving swing	(iii)	Periodic motion

Ans. The correct matching is as given

(a)—(ii), (b)—(i), (c)-(iii)

(a) Rotational motion is a motion in a circular path about a fixed axis.

(b) Circular motion is a motion of an object or a part of it around a fixed point.

(c) Periodic motion is the motion that repeats itself after some period of time.

Long Answer Type Questions

Q. 17 While travelling in a train, it appears that the trees near the track are moving whereas co-passengers appear to be stationary. Explain the reason.

Ans. While travelling, trees near the track seem to be moving back (i.e. opposite to the direction of motion of a train) because there is a relative motion between the outside trees and the moving train.

While in case of co-passengers, the relative motion between us and co-passengers, is zero, so they appear to be stationary.

Q. 18 How are the motions of a wheel of a moving bicycle and a mark on the blade of a moving electric fan different? Explain.

Ans. Differences between wheel of moving bicycle and mark on the blade of electric fan are as given:

Wheel of moving bicycle	Mark on the blade of electric fan
It executes rectilinear as well as circular motion because the wheel as a whole will move forward and its point or particles around the rim will execute circular motion.	It executes circular motion because the mark on the blade of a fan will move such that its distance from the centre of the fan will remain same.
It changes position while executing circular motion.	It cannot change its position.
It can cover some distances in any time interval.	It cannot cover any distance.
Wheel around its axle executes rotational motion.	It cannot execute rotational motion.

Q. 19 Three students measured the length of a corridor and reported their measurements. The values of their measurements were different. What could be the reason for difference in their measurements?

(Mention any three)

Ans.   The reasons may be as follows:

(i) Their scales of measurement may not be standard or they may be using different scales of measurement.

(ii) The length of the scale may not be proper, i.e. the length of scale may be shorter than the length they want to measure.

(iii) There may be some errors in the scale which they are using or they may not be using the correct method of observing the scale.

Q. 20 Boojho was riding in his bicycle along a straight road. He classified the motion of various parts of the bicycle as (a) rectilinear motion (b) circular motion and (c) both rectilinear as well as circular motion. Can you list one part of the bicycle for each type of motion? Support your answer with reason.

Ans.   (a) **Rectilinear motion** The handle of bicycle will always move in rectilinear path because it cannot execute circular or rotatory motion.

(b) **Circular motion** The pedals of bicycle will always move circularly around its chain fixing system because they cannot move in forward direction without the whole chain system.

(c) **Both rectilinear and circular** The wheels of bicycle will move in rectilinear as well as in circular motion because the wheel as a whole will move forward and its point or particles around the rim will execute circular motion.

11

Light

Multiple Choice Questions (MCQs)

Q. 1 Observe the picture given in the figure carefully.

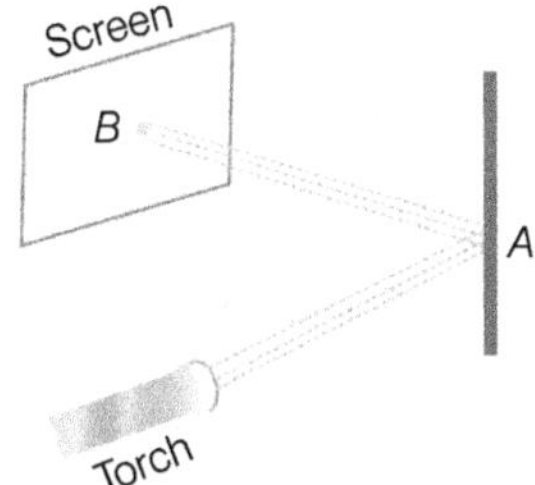

A patch of light is obtained at *B* when the torch is lighted as shown. Which of the following is kept at position *A* to get this patch of light?

(a) A wooden board
(b) A glass sheet
(c) A mirror
(d) A sheet of white paper

Ans. *(c)* A mirror is kept at position *A* to get a patch of light because only a mirror can change the direction of light that falls on it, i.e. causes reflection.

Q. 2 Four students *A, B, C* and *D* looked through pipes of different shapes to see a candle flame as shown in figure.

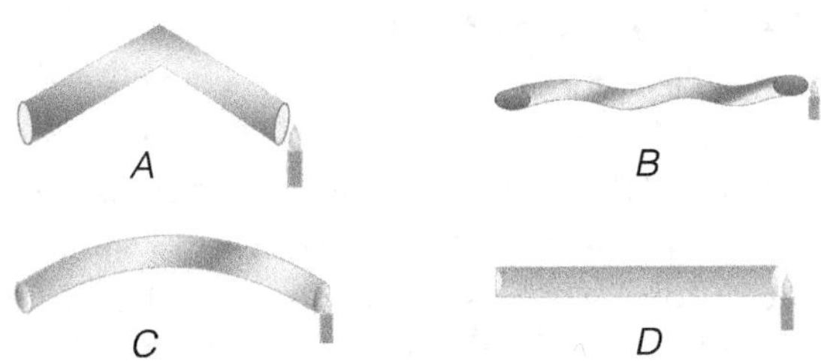

Who will be able to see the candle flame clearly?

(a) *A*
(b) *B*
(c) *C*
(d) *D*

Ans. *(d)* Student *D* will be able to see the candle flame clearly because light travels along a straight line. However, students *A, B* and *C* will not be able to see the flame clearly because the tubes are not straight.

Q. 3 A student observes a tree given in figure through a pinhole camera. Which of the diagrams given in figure (a) to (d) depicts the image seen by her correctly?

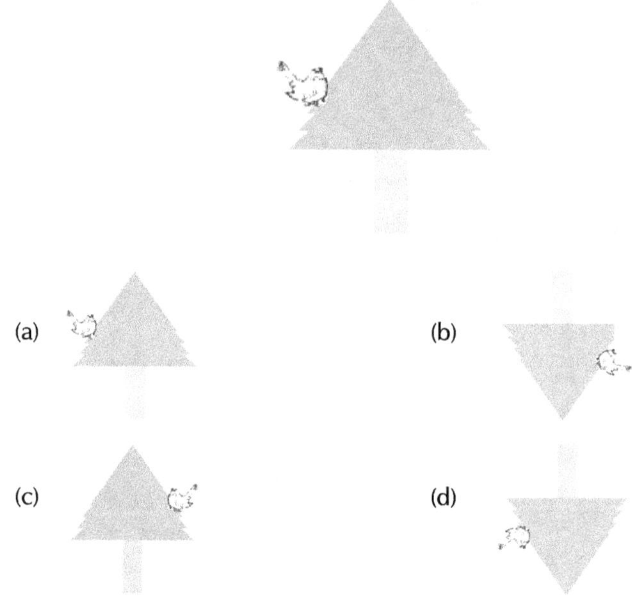

Ans. *(d)* Option (d) is the correct image seen by her because a pinhole camera always forms upside down (i.e. inverted) image.

Q. 4 Which of the following is/are not always necessary to observe a shadow?

    (a) Sun   (b) Screen   (c) Source of light   (d) Opaque object

Ans. *(a)* Sun is not always necessary to observe a shadow because any source of light, an opaque object and a screen are just necessary enough to see a shadow.

Q. 5 Paheli observed the shadow of a tree at 8:00 am, 12:00 noon and 3:00 pm. Which of the following statements is closest to her observation about the shape and size of the shadow?

    (a) The shape of the shadow of the tree changes but the size remains the same.

    (b) The size of the shadow of the tree changes but the shape remains the same.

    (c) Both the size and shape of the shadow of the tree changes.

    (d) Neither the shape nor the size of the shadow changes.

Ans. *(c)* Both the size and shape of the shadow of the tree will be changed because at 8:00 am and 3:00 pm, the lengths of the shadows of tree will be longer than its actual length and point to the West and the East directions, respectively. However, at 12:00 noon, the sun will be high in the sky just above the tree, so the shadow of tree will be short.

Q. 6 Which of the following can never form a circular shadow?

    (a) A ball   (b) A flat disc

    (c) A shoe box   (d) An ice-cream cone

Ans. *(c)* A shoe box can never form a circular shadow because in any condition it does not have a circular shape. However, a ball, a flat disc and the base of ice-cream cone can form a circular shadow.

Q. 7 Two students while sitting across a table looked down onto its top surface. They noticed that they could see their own and each other's image. The table top is likely to be made of

    (a) unpolished wood   (b) red stone

    (c) glass sheet   (d) wood top covered with cloth

Ans. *(c)* The table top must be made of glass sheet because only a glass sheet can show the images of both the students, which can be seen by both of them.

Very Short Answer Type Questions

Q. 8 You have 3 opaque strips with very small holes of different shapes as shown in figure. If you obtain an image of the sun on a wall through these holes, will the image formed by these holes be the same or different?

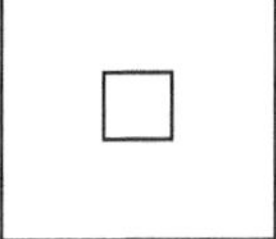  

Ans. A small circular image of the sun will be obtained in all the three cases because the holes will act as a pinhole camera, whatever be their shapes. Also, as the light moves in a straight path, therefore the image of the sun will remain same.

Q. 9 Observe the picture given in figure. A sheet of some material is placed at position *P*, still the patch of light is obtained on the screen. What is the type of material of this sheet?

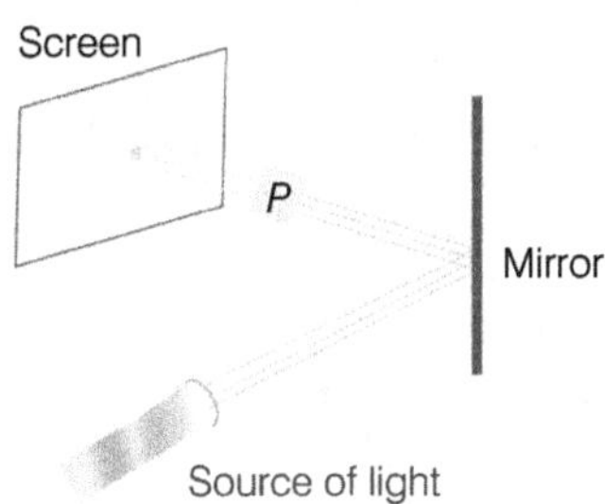

Ans. A sheet of transparent material is placed at position *P* because only a transparent material allows light to pass through it undisturbed and therefore, the patch of light is obtained at the same place on the screen.

Q. 10 Three torches *A*, *B* and *C* shown in figure are switched ON one by one. The light from which of the torch will not form a shadow of the ball on the screen?

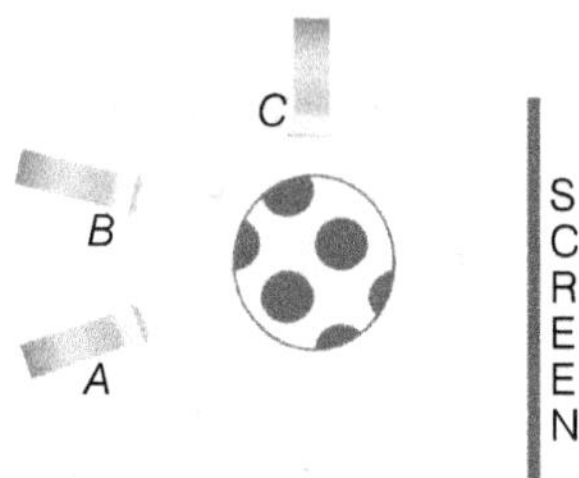

Ans. The light from the torch *C* will not form a shadow on the screen because light travels in a straight path and forms the shadow on the same path from which it is coming.

Q. 11 Look at the given figure.

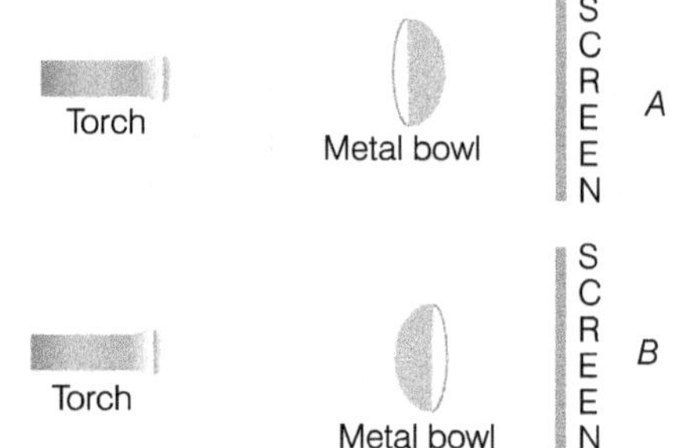

Will there be any difference in the shadow formed on the screen *A* and *B*?

Ans. No, there will not be any difference because the length and breadth of an object are same in both the cases.

Short Answer Type Questions

Q. 12 Correct the following statements.

    (a) The colour of the shadow of an object depends on its colour.

    (b) Transparent objects allow light to pass through them partially.

Ans. (a) The colour of the shadow of an object does not depend on its colour. It is always black irrespective of any coloured object.

    (b) Transparent objects allow most of the light to pass through them or translucent objects allow light to pass through them partially.

Q. 13 Suggest a situation where we obtain more than one shadow of an object at a time.

Ans. More than one shadow or multiple shadows of an object can be obtained by using multiple sources of light, i.e. during a night match being played in a stadium, multiple shadows of players are seen due to flood (stadium) lights in the stadium.

Q. 14 On a sunny day, does a bird or an aeroplane flying high in the sky cast its shadow on the ground? Under what circumstances, can we see their shadow on the ground?

Ans. No, they do not cast any shadow on the ground because they are very high in the sky. They can cast shadow only if they are at some lower height, i.e. if they are near to the ground, we can see their shadows.

Q. 15 You are given a transparent glass sheet. Suggest any two ways to make it translucent without breaking it.

Ans. Transparent glass sheet can be made translucent by two ways :

    (i) By rubbing it on the ground and making it rough.

    (ii) By applying oil, grease or butter on it.

Q. 16 A torch is placed at two different positions A and B one by one as shown in figure.

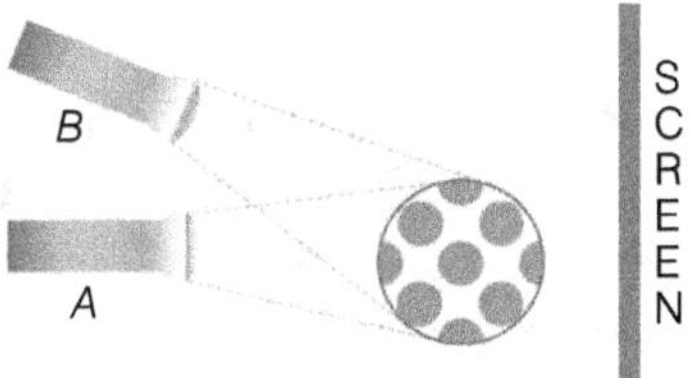

The shape of the shadow obtained in two positions is shown in the given figure.

(a)   (b)

Match the position of the torch and shape of the shadow of the ball.

Ans. Position A of the torch will form the shadow (a) and position B of the torch will form the shadow (b) of the football. Here, difference in shapes of shadows (a) and (b) of ball is due to the difference in the positions A and B of torch from the ball.

The bigger shape of shadow (a) than shadow (b) of ball is formed only because the screen, torch in position A and ball are in same straight line.

Q. 17 A student covered a torch with red cellophone sheet to obtain red light. Using the red light, she obtains a shadow of an opaque object. She repeats this activity with green and blue lights. Will the colour of the light affect the shadow? Explain.

Ans. Shadow is just an absence of light at that place. Shadow is not affected by the colours of the object because the amount of light preventing to pass will remain same.

The shadow is affected by the shape of the object only. If the object is large, the shadow will be large and *vice-versa*.

Q. 18 Is air around us always transparent? Discuss.

Ans. We can see the objects through air clearly, means we can observe all the objects in their original shapes and sizes without any disturbance, it means the environment around us which is just air, must be transparent.

But when thick smoke, thick clouds, etc., are present in the air, it does not remain transparent.

Q. 19 Three identical towels of red, blue and green colour are hanging on a clothe's line in the sun. What would be the colour of shadows of these towels?

Ans. Shadow of an object does not change on changing its colour. Shadow will always show the absence of light at that place. So, the colour of shadow will remain same in all the cases. Thus, the shadows of all the towels are black in colour.

Q. 20 Using a pinhole camera, a student observes the image of two of his friends, standing in sunlight, wearing yellow and red shirts, respectively. What will be the colours of the shirts in the image?

Ans. Colours of the shirts will remain same. We see them on the screen because pinhole camera forms the image of the object having same colour but upside down.

So, yellow shirt will form yellow image and red shirt will form red image.

Q. 21 In given figure, a flower made of thick coloured paper has been pasted on the transparent glass sheet. What will be the shape and colour of shadow seen on the screen?

Ans. The shape of the flower on the screen will be the same as that of the flower but the shadow of flower is of black colour.

Long Answer Type Questions

Q. 22 A football match is being played at night in a stadium with flood lights ON. You can see the shadow of a football kept at the ground but cannot see its shadow when it is kicked high in the air. Explain.

Ans. The shadow of an object cannot be caught if the screen and the object are very far from each other. This is the same case. Here, also the shadow of the football cannot be seen on the ground (which acts as a screen) when it is kicked high in the air.

This happens because if we take the object away and away from the screen, the shadow becomes smaller and smaller in size and a time comes when it totally disappears from the screen.

Q. 23 A student had a ball, a screen and a torch in working condition. He tried to form a shadow of the ball on the screen by placing them at different positions. Sometimes, the shadow was not obtained. Explain.

Ans. Sometimes, the shadow of the object (ball) may not be formed because of improper arrangement of source of light (torch), object and screen. It may be due to the following reasons— (a) The screen from the ball. (b) The direction of beam of light from the torch falling on the ball, is parallel to the screen. (c) The torch is kept away from the ball.

An accurate shadow of ball will be formed only if screen, torch and ball are in the same straight line (as shown in figure).

Q. 24 A sheet of plywood, a piece of muslin cloth and that of a transparent glass, all of the same size and shape were placed at *A* one by one in the arrangement shown in figure. Will the shadow be formed in each case? If yes, then how will the shadow on the screen be different in each case? Give reasons for your answer.

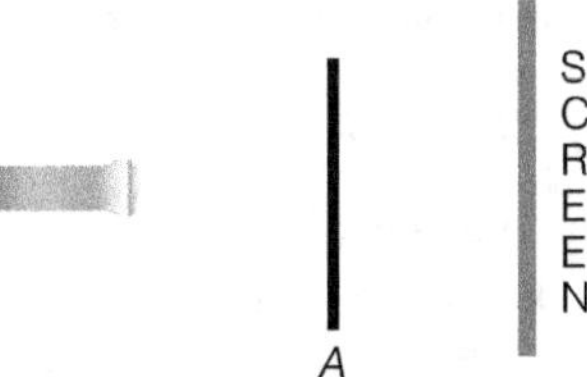

Ans. Yes, the shadow will be formed in each case but in all the cases, the darkness of the shadow will be different.

(i) Most of the light in case of transparent sheet of glass will pass through the glass. So, the darkness of shadow will be very low.

(ii) Most of the light in case of muslin cloth will be reflected. So, the shadow will be darker than the transparent sheet of glass.

(iii) While in case of plywood, all the light would be stopped completely by the plywood. So, the darkness strength will be highest in this case.

12

Electricity and Circuits

Multiple Choice Questions (MCQs)

Q. 1 Choose from the options (a), (b), (c) and (d) given below the figure which shows the correct direction of current.

Ans. *(b)* Current always starts from positive terminal and end at negative terminal of the battery. This is conventional direction of flow of current in a circuit.

Q. 2 Choose the incorrect statement.

(a) A switch is the source of electric current in a circuit

(b) A switch helps to complete or break the circuit

(c) A switch helps us to use electricity as per our requirement

(d) When the switch is open, there is an air gap between its terminals

Ans. *(a)* A switch cannot be a source of electric current in the circuit. Electric cell is a source of electricity in the circuit. Other options are the functions of a switch.

Q. 3 In an electric bulb, light is produced due to the glowing of

(a) the glass case of the bulb   (b) the thin filament

(c) the thick wires supporting the filament   (d) gases inside glass case of the bulb

Ans. *(b)* In an electric bulb, its thin filament glows and gives off light and heat.

Q. 4 In the following arrangement shown in figure, the bulb will not glow if the ends *A* and *B* are connected with

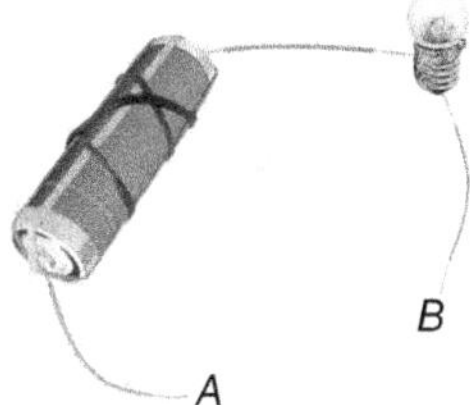

(a) a steel spoon   (b) a metal clip   (c) a plastic clip   (d) a copper wire

Ans. *(c)* Since, a plastic clip is an insulator, so current will not pass through it and bulb will not glow in this case. However, a steel spoon, a metal clip and a copper wire are conductors of electricity.

Q. 5 In the circuit shown in figure, when the switch is moved to ON position, then

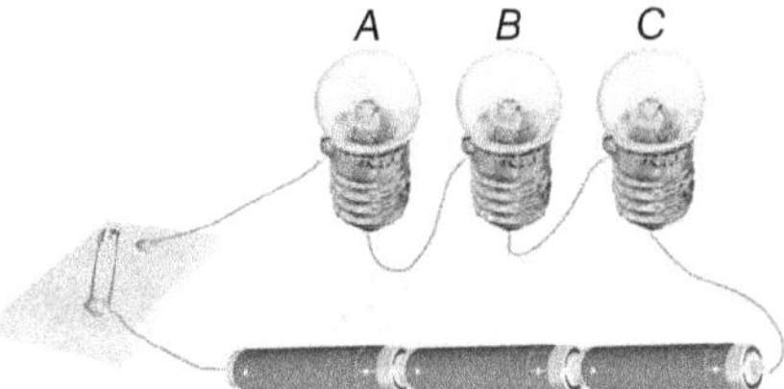

(a) the bulb *A* will glow first   (b) the bulb *B* will glow first
(c) the bulb *C* will glow first   (d) all bulbs will glow together

Ans. *(d)* All the bulbs will glow together because current will reach simultaneously to all the bulbs, when the switch is moved to ON position.

Q. 6 Filament of a torch bulb is

(a) a metal case
(b) metal tip at the centre of the base
(c) two thick wires
(d) a thin wire

Ans. *(d)* Filament of a torch bulb is a thin wire which gives off light. It is fixed to two thicker wires which provides support to it.

One of these thick wires is connected to the metal case at the base of the bulb and the other thick wire is connected to the metal tip at the centre of the base.

Q. 7 Paheli is running short of connecting wires. To complete an electric circuit, she may use a

(a) glass bangle   (b) thick thread
(c) rubber pipe   (d) steel spoon

Ans. *(d)* Since, a steel spoon is a conductor of electricity therefore, current will pass through it. So, Paheli can use a steel spoon to complete the circuit.

Very Short Answer Type Questions

Q. 8 In which of the following circuits *A*, *B* and *C* given in figure, the cell will be used up very rapidly?

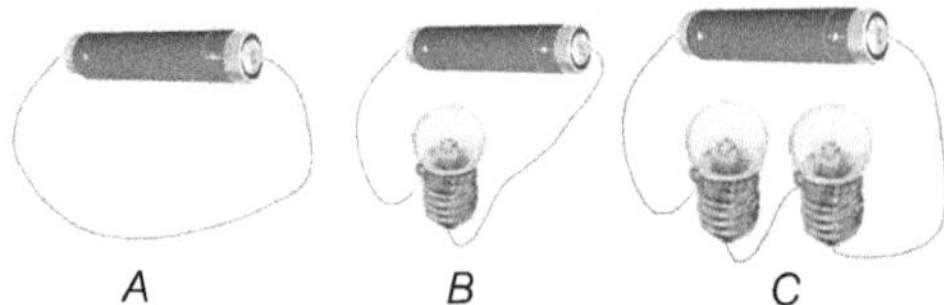

Ans. The cell will be used up rapidly in *A* because all the current will discharge through the wire very rapidly as no appliance is connected between the positive and negative terminals of the cell.

Q. 9 Figure shows a bulb with its different parts marked as 1, 2, 3, 4 and 5. Which of them label the terminals of the bulb?

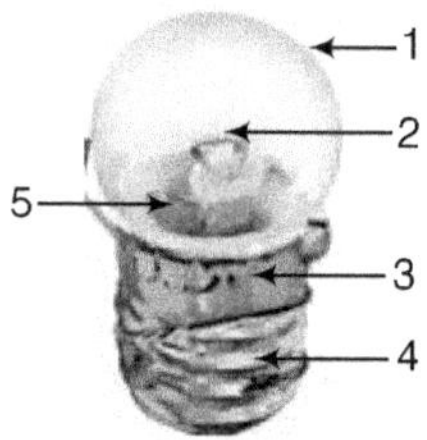

Ans. 1 → Glass covering   2 → Filament

3 → Terminal   4 → Terminal

5 → Base wires (supporting filament)

As from the question, labels 3 and 4 are the terminals of the bulb.

Short Answer Type Questions

Q. 10 You are provided with a bulb, a cell, a switch and some connecting wires. Draw a diagram to show the connections between them to make the bulb glow.

Ans. The complete circuit diagram so that the bulb glows is given below:

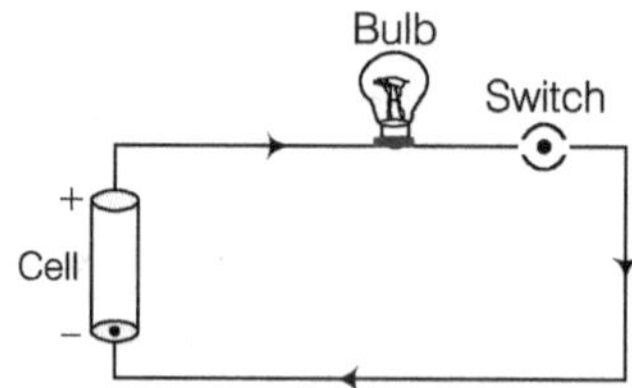

Q. 11 Will the bulb glow in the circuit shown in figure? Explain.

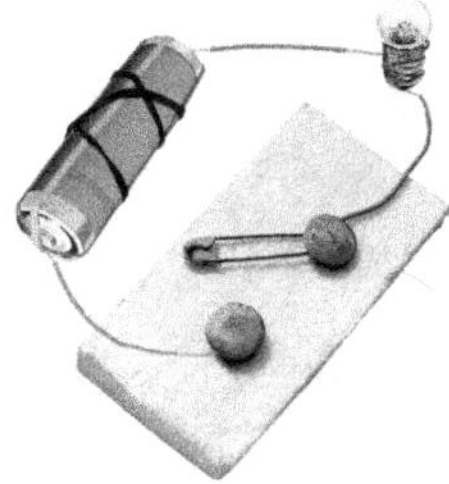

Ans. As in the given circuit diagram, it seems that the switch is open, i.e. there is an air gap between the connecting wires, so the circuit is not complete and therefore, the bulb will not glow.

Q. 12 An electric bulb is connected to a cell through a switch as shown in figure. When the switch is brought in ON position, the bulb does not glow. What could be the possible reasons for it? Mention any two of them.

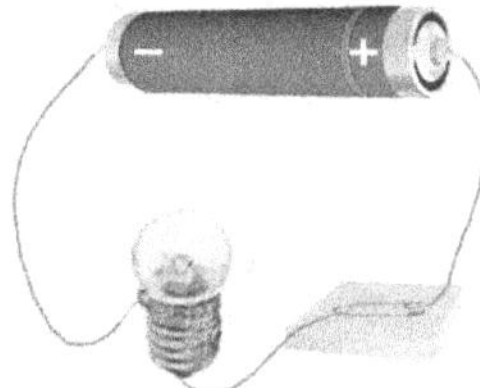

Ans. The possible reasons so that even at switch ON position the bulb is not glowing are:
   (i) The cell may be discharged.
   (ii) The bulb may be fused.
   (iii) The wire may be broken from inside.
   (iv) The connections may be loose.

Q. 13 A torch requires 3 cells. Show the arrangement of the cells with a diagram inside the torch so that the bulb glows.

Ans. The arrangement of bulb should be such that the positive terminal of a battery touches the base of the bulb. When switched ON, the bulb will glow.

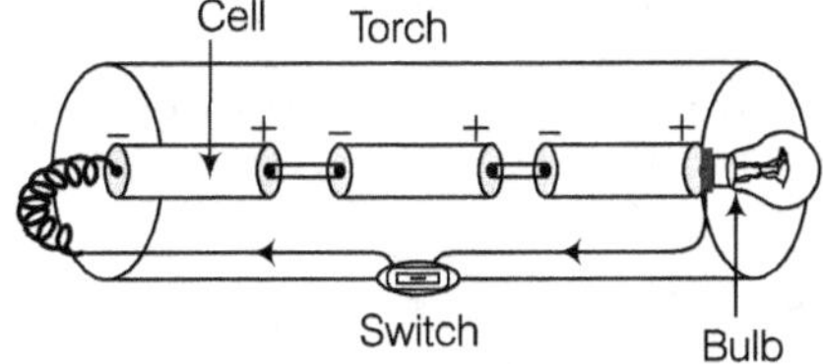

Q. 14 When the chemicals in the electric cell are used up, the electric cell stops producing electricity. The electric cell is then replaced with a new one. In case of rechargeable batteries (such as the type used in mobile phones, cameras and inverters), they are used again and again. How?

Ans. A rechargeable battery has such chemicals which on after usage can be restored, by passing a suitable current in the opposite direction to the rechargeable battery, so that it can be used again and again.

Q. 15 Paheli connected two bulbs to a cell as shown in figure.

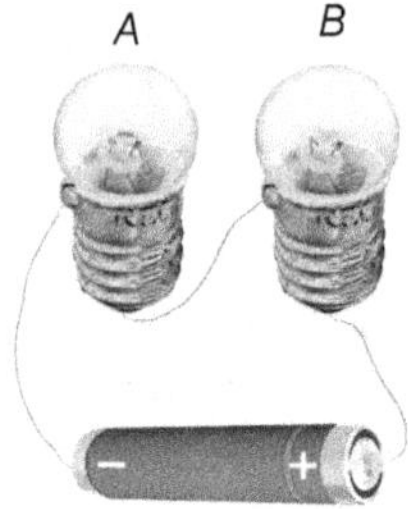

She found that filament of bulb *B* is broken. Will the bulb *A* glow in this circuit? Give reason.

Ans. No, the bulb *A* will not glow in the circuit because the filament of the bulb *B* is broken and the current will not pass through it, i.e. the circuit is broken or incomplete. Therefore, the current will not flow in the whole circuit.

Q. 16 Why do bulbs have two terminals?

Ans. Bulb has two terminals to connect the filament with the terminals of a cell or a battery so that the current can pass through the filament.

Q. 17 Which of the following arrangement *A, B, C* and *D* given in figure should not be set up? Explain why.

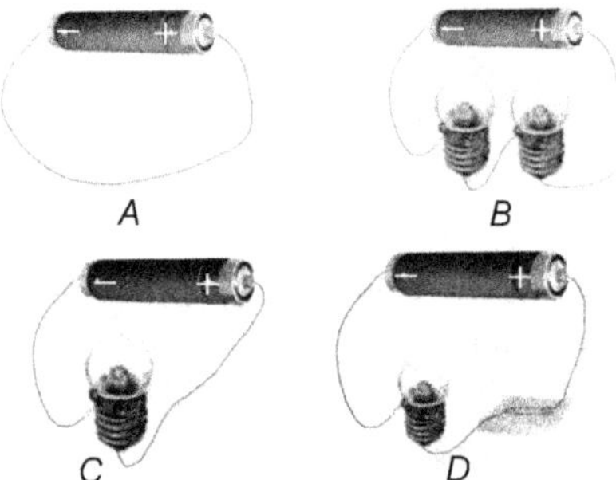

Ans. Arrangement *A* should not be set up because in this arrangement cell will be used up very rapidly as no appliance is connected between the two terminals of the cell.

Q. 18 A fused bulb does not glow. Why?

Ans. A fused bulb does not glow because in a fused bulb, the filament is broken and the circuit is incomplete. Therefore, the current does not flow through it.

Q. 19 Paheli wanted to glow a torch bulb using a cell. She could not get connecting wires, instead, she got two strips of aluminium foil. Will she succeed? Explain how.

Ans. Yes, she will succeed. Aluminium foils can act as connecting wires because aluminium is a conductor of electricity, it will complete the circuit and therefore, the bulb will glow.

Long Answer Type Questions

Q. 20 Boojho has a cell and a single piece of connecting wire. Without cutting the wire in two, will he be able to make the bulb glow? Explain with the help of a circuit diagram.

Ans. Yes, this can be done by arranging the circuit as given below:

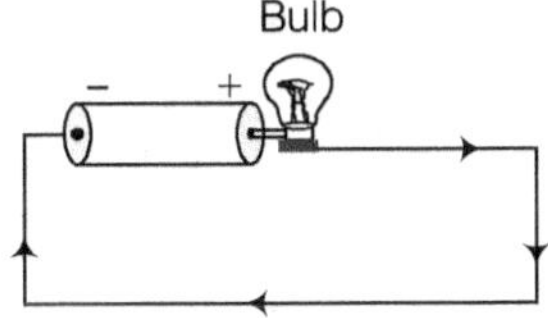

In this arrangement, one terminal of the bulb should be connected directly to the positive (say) terminal of the cell and the other terminal of the bulb should be connected to the negative terminal of the cell using the given piece of connecting wire.

Q. 21 Figures *A* and *B* show a bulb connected to a cell in two different ways.

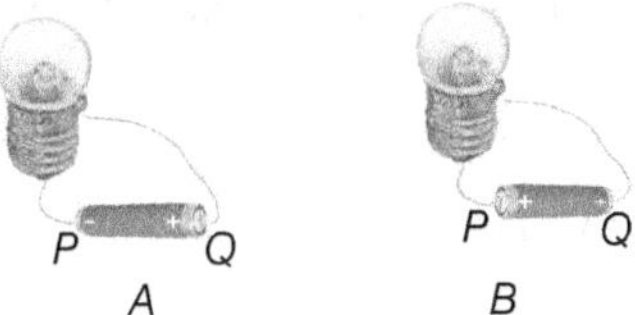

 (a) What will be the direction of the current through the bulb in both the cases (*Q* to *P* or *P* to *Q*)?

 (b) Will the bulb glow in both the cases?

 (c) Does the brightness of the glowing bulb depend on the direction of current through it?

Ans. (a) The direction of current will be from *Q* to *P* in *A* and direction of current will be from *P* to *Q* in *B*. This is because the direction of current is always from positive terminal to negative terminal of the cell or battery. This is the conventional direction of flow of current in the circuit.

 (b) Yes, the bulb will glow in both the cases because for the bulb to glow, we just need to complete the circuit.

 (c) No, the brightness of the bulb never depends upon the direction of current passing through it.

Q. 22 Think of six activities which use electric current. Also name the devices used to perform the activity.

	Activity you perform	Device
1.	Get light	Torch
2.	....	....
3.	....	....
4.	....	....
5.	....	....
6.	....	....

Ans. The name of the devices and their activity are as given:

	Activity you perform	Device
1.	Get light	Torch
2.	Get the moving air	Fan
3.	Get the mechanical work	Motor
4.	Get the hot water	Geyser
5.	Get the cold water	Refrigerator
6.	Get the live match or movies	Television

Q. 23 A torch is not functioning, though contact points in the torch are in working condition. What can be the possible reasons for this? Mention any three.

Ans. The possible reasons for not functioning of torch are:

(i) The torch bulb may be fused.

(ii) The cells may be discharged.

(iii) The connecting wires may be broken up.

(iv) The cells may not be placed in the correct order.

(v) The switch is faulty.

13

Fun with Magnets

Multiple Choice Questions (MCQs)

Q. 1 Observe the pictures *A* and *B* given in figure carefully.

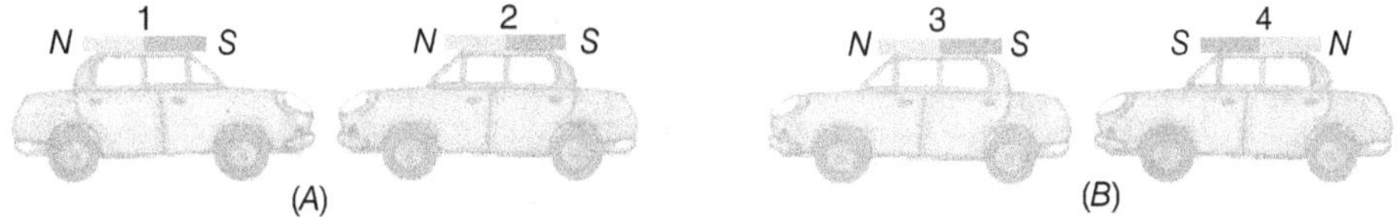

Which of the following statements is correct for the above given pictures?

(a) In *A*, cars 1 and 2 will come closer and in *B*, cars 3 and 4 will come closer.

(b) In *A*, cars 1 and 2 will move away from each other and in *B*, cars 3 and 4 will move away.

(c) In *A*, cars 1 and 2 will move away and in *B*, 3 and 4 will come closer to each other.

(d) In *A*, cars 1 and 2 will come closer to each other and in *B*, 3 and 4 will move away from each other.

Ans. *(d)* In *A*, cars 1 and 2 will come closer to each other because North and South poles (i.e. opposite poles) attract each other while in *B*, cars 3 and 4 will move away from each other because South poles (i.e. similar poles) repel each other.s

Q. 2 The arrangement to store two magnets is shown by figures (a), (b), (c) and (d) in figure. Which one of them is the correct arrangement?

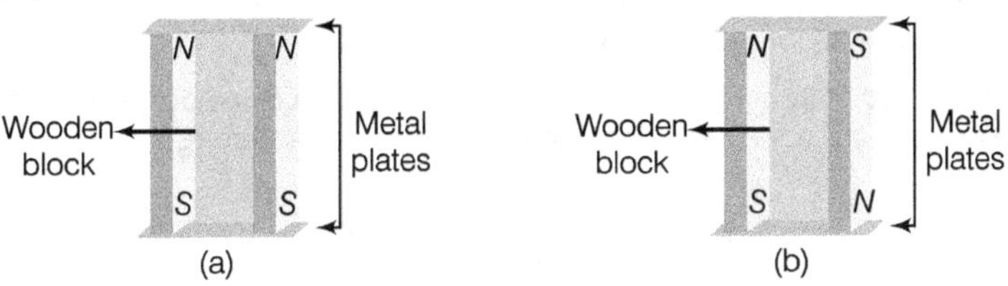

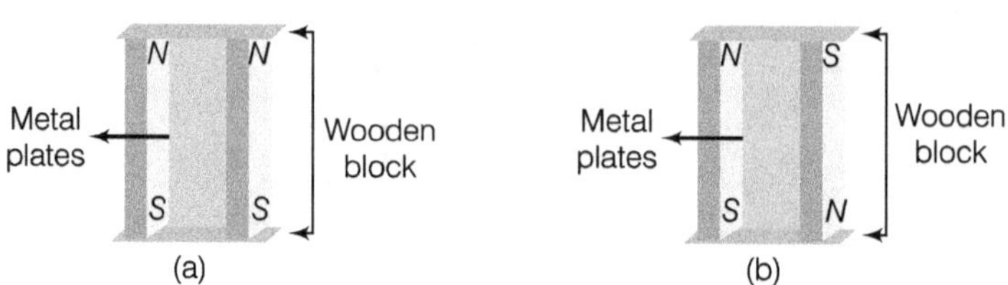

Ans. *(b)* The correct arrangement is shown in option (b). To store the two magnets safely, they should be kept in pairs with their unlike poles on the same side. They must be separated by a piece of wood, while two metal plates should be placed across their ends.

Q. 3 Three magnets *A, B* and *C* were dipped one by one in a heap of iron filings. Figure shows the amount of the iron filings sticking to them.

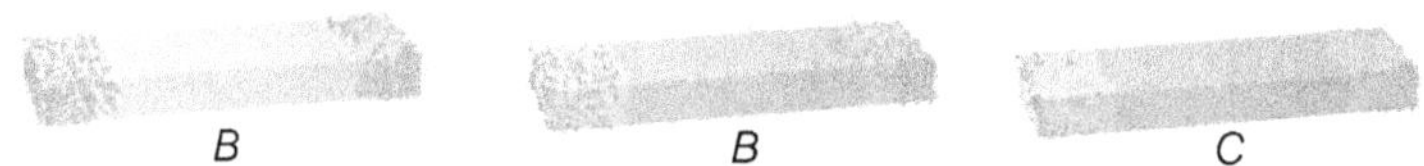

The strength of these magnets will be

(a) $A > B > C$ (b) $A < B < C$

(c) $A = B = C$ (d) $A < B > C$

Ans. *(a)* As we can see from the diagram that amount of iron filings in *A* is greater than *B* and *C* and in *B*, it is greater than *C*. So, the strength of magnets will be according to the amount of iron filings sticking to them only.

Q. 4 North pole of a magnet can be identified by

(a) another magnet having its poles marked as North Pole and South pole

(b) another magnet no matter whether the poles are marked or not

(c) using an iron bar

(d) using iron filings

Ans. *(a)* North pole (South pole) can be identified only if we have another magnet having its poles marked as North pole and South pole because only then we can see the attraction and repulsion between *N-S* (i.e. opposite) poles and *N-N* (i.e. similar) poles, respectively.

Q. 5 A bar magnet is immersed in a heap of iron filings and pulled out. The amount of iron filings clinging to the

(a) North pole is almost equal to the South pole

(b) North pole is much more than the South pole

(c) North pole is much less than the South pole

(d) magnet will be same all along its length

Ans. *(a)* The amount of iron filings clinging to the North pole is almost equal to the South pole because in a magnet, the strength of both the poles is same.

Very Short Answer Type Questions

Q. 6 Fill in the blanks

    (i) When a bar magnet is broken, each of the broken part will have ...... pole/poles.

    (ii) In a bar magnet, magnetic attraction is ...... near its ends.

Ans. (i) Two; When a bar magnet is broken, each of the broken part will behave as a magnet having two magnetic poles, North and South.

    (ii) Strong; In a bar magnet, magnetic attraction or its strength is maximum at poles and minimum at the centre.

Q. 7 Paheli and her friends were decorating the class bulletin board. She dropped the box of stainless steel pins by mistake. She tried to collect the pins using a magnet. She could not succeed. What could be the reason for this?

Ans. She could not succeed because the stainless steel pins are not made of iron, i.e. they are non-magnetic, so they are not attracted towards magnet.

Q. 8 How will you test that 'tea dust' is not adulterated with iron powder?

Ans. We can do a simple experiment for this:

    (i) Take tea dust on a paper.

    (ii) Take a bar magnet in your hand.

    (iii) Place the bar magnet over this dust.

    (iv) If some particles are attracted strongly towards this magnet by clinging to it, then definitely tea dust will have iron powder.

Q. 9 Boojho dipped a bar magnet in a heap of iron filings and pulled it out. He found that iron filings got stuck to the magnet as shown in figure.

    (a) Which regions of the magnet have more iron filings sticking to it?

    (b) What are these regions called?

Ans. (a) The two ends of the magnet have more iron filings sticking to it because magnetic strength is maximum near the ends of the magnet.

    (b) These ends are called poles of the magnet (i.e. North and South poles of magnet).

Short Answer Type Questions

Q. 10 Four identical iron bars were dipped in a heap of iron filings one by one. Figure shows the amount of iron filings sticking to each of them.

(i)   (ii)   (iii)   (iv)

(a) Which of the iron bar is likely to be the strongest magnet?

(b) Which of the iron bar is not a magnet? Justify your answer.

Ans. (a) Iron bar (i) seems to be the strongest magnet because the maximum amount of iron filings are sticking to it, i.e. maximum iron filings have been attracted by it.

(b) Iron bar (ii) is not a magnet because no iron filings have been attracted by it.

Q. 11 A toy car has a bar magnet laid hidden inside its body along its length. Using another magnet, how will you find out which pole of the magnet is facing the front of the car?

Ans. If we face North pole of a magnet towards the front side of the car and the car is attracted, it means its front side pole is South pole and if it is going away, it means its front side is North pole.

Q. 12 Match the Column I with Column II (one option of I can match with more than one option of II).

	Column I		Column II
(a)	Magnet attracts	(i)	rests along a particular direction
(b)	Magnet can be repelled	(ii)	iron
(c)	Magnet if suspended freely	(iii)	by another magnet
(d)	Poles of the magnet can be identified by	(iv)	iron filings

Ans. (a)– (ii), (iii) and (iv)

A magnet can attract magnetic materials like iron, iron filings and another magnet.

(b)– (iii)

If the North pole of a magnet is brought near the North pole of another magnet, then they both repel each other. Similarly, S-S poles of two magnets repel each other.

(c)– (i)

A magnet always stops in a particular direction (N-S), if suspended freely from a thread from its centre.

(d)– (iii)

Poles of a magnet can be identified only if we have another magnet having its poles marked as North pole and South pole because only then we can see the attraction and repulsion between *N-S* poles and *N-N* poles, respectively.

Q. 13 You are provided with two identical metal bars. One out of the two, is a magnet. Suggest two ways to identify the magnet.

Ans. The two ways to identify the magnet are

(i) Suspend the metal bars having their levels horizontal with a thread one by one. Let the metal bar come to rest.
Now, if we move it by pushing it slowly in any direction, then it will return to the same direction. This means that it is a magnet otherwise it is simply an iron bar.

(ii) Take some iron filings and move the iron bars over these iron filings one by one. If iron filings are attracted very strongly at poles, then it is a magnet and if they are not attracted, then it is simply an iron bar.

Long Answer Type Questions

Q. 14 Three identical iron bars are kept on a table. Two out of three bars are magnets. In one of the magnets the North-South poles are marked. How will you find out which of the other two bars is a magnet? Identify the poles of this magnet.

Ans. To find out the magnet:

(i) Take the bar magnet with known poles in your hand.

(ii) Take one of the other two iron bars in other hand.

(iii) Bring one side of iron bar towards the South pole of the bar magnet and note down whether it is attracted or repelled.

(iv) Bring other side of iron bar towards the South pole of the bar magnet and again note down the same thing.

(v) If there is an attraction in both cases (iii) and (iv), then it is definitely a simple iron bar.

(vi) If there is an attraction in one case and repulsion in other case, then it is a bar magnet.

(vii) Do the same for the third iron bar.

To find out the poles:

If in case (iii), the bar is attracted, then it is North pole of the identified bar magnet. If the bar is repelled, then it is obviously a South pole of the identified bar magnet.

Q. 15 Describe the steps involved in magnetising an iron strip with the help of a magnet.

Ans. Steps involved in magnetising an iron strip are:

(i) Take an iron strip which is to be magnetised.

(ii) Keep it on a wooden table.

(iii) Hold one end of a bar magnet in your hand and keep the other end of bar magnet near one edge of iron strip.

(iv) Without lifting, move it along the length of iron strip till you reach the other edge.

(v) After reaching the end of iron strip, lift the bar magnet and bring it to the same position and repeat the process again and again.

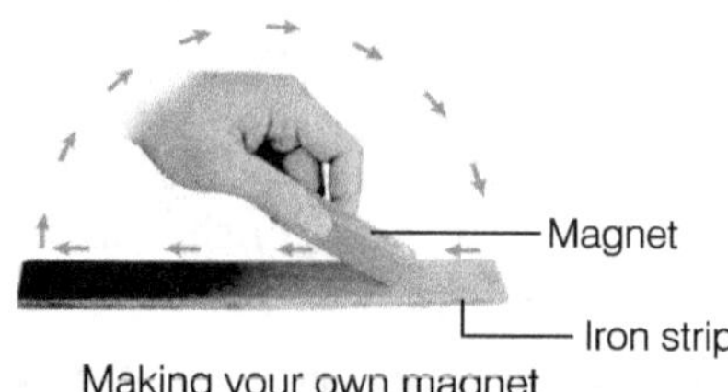

Making your own magnet

(vi) Bring some iron filings near the iron strip to check whether it has become a magnet. If not, continue the same process for some more time.

Q. 16 Given below is a figure which shows a magnetic campass. Briefly explain what will happen to the position of its needle if you bring a bar magnet near it? Also, draw a diagram to show the effect on the needle on bringing the bar magnet near it. Also, draw the diagram to show the effect when the other end of the bar magnet is brought near it.

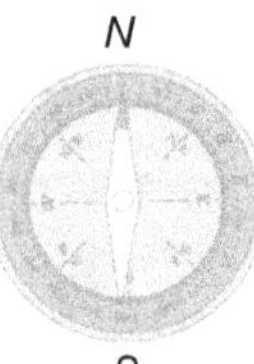

Ans. If we bring a bar magnet near a magnetic compass N, its needle will get deflected.

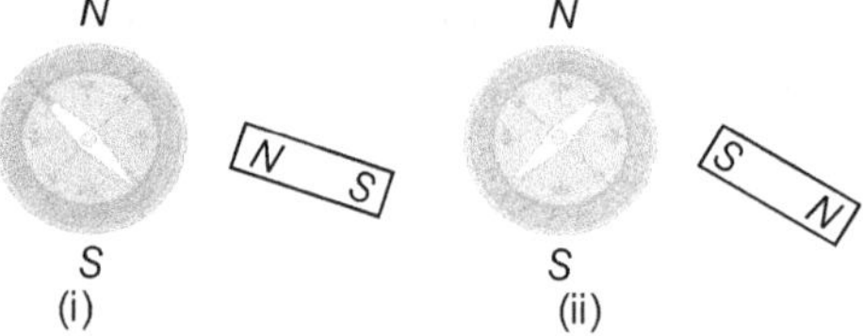

When we bring North pole of a bar magnet near the magnetic compass, its needle will be deflected away from the magnet as shown in Fig. (i). However, when we bring South pole of bar magnet near the magnetic compass, needle will be deflected towards the magnet as shown in Fig. (ii).

Q. 17 Suggest an activity to prepare a magnetic compass by using an iron needle and a bar magnet.

Ans. Steps involved in preparing a magnetic compass are :

(i) Take an iron needle which is to be magnetised.

(ii) Magnetise it using a bar magnet.

(iii) Insert the magnetised needle through a small piece of cork.

(iv) Let the cork float in a water in a bowl. Make sure that the needle does not touch the water.

(v) Your magnetic compass is now ready to work. Note the direction in which the needle points when the cork is floating.

(vi) Rotate the cork, with the needle fixed in it, in different directions. Note the direction in which the needle points when the cork begins to float again without rotating.

You will observe that the needle indicates the North-South direction when it comes to rest.

Q. 18 Boojho kept a magnet close to an ordinary iron bar. He observed that the iron bar attracts a pin as shown in figure.

What inference could he draw from this observation? Explain.

Ans. When we place any iron bar near a bar magnet, the magnetic properties are induced in it and it acts like a magnet. The small objects like pin, iron filings can be attracted by it. But when we remove the bar magnet kept near it, it again becomes an iron bar and does not attract the small iron objects.

Q. 19 A bar magnet is cut into two pieces *A* and *B* from the middle as shown in figure.

Will the two pieces act as individual magnets? Mark the poles of these two pieces. Suggest an activity to verify your answer.

Ans.

Yes, the two pieces will work as individual magnets because a monopole (single pole) of magnet never exists.

Activity

(i) Place the magnet, so formed (*A* and *B*) on the table.

(ii) Bring the North pole of both magnets towards each other, they will be repelled.

(iii) Bring the North and South poles of both magnets towards each other, they will attract.

This proves that the two pieces will act as individual magnets having attraction and repulsion properties.

Q. 20 Suggest an arrangement to store a U-shaped magnet. How is this different from storing a pair of bar magnets?

Ans. It is a suggested way shown in figure below :

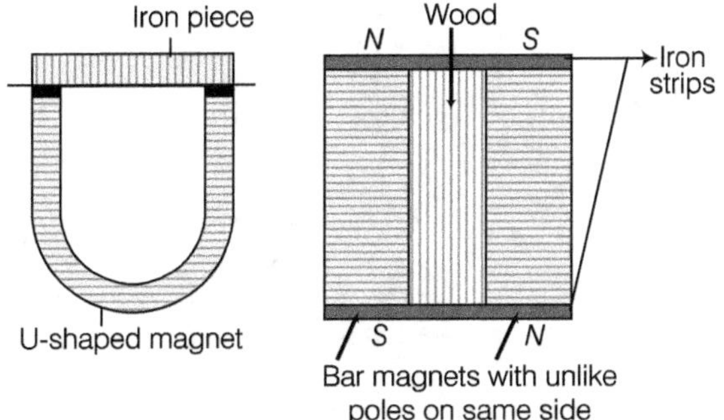

U-shaped magnet is kept along with an iron piece across its two poles, while a pair of bar magnets is kept along with iron strips and magnets separated by wood along their length as shown in above figure.

14

Water

Multiple Choice Questions (MCQs)

Q. 1 Which of the following activities does not involve use of water?

    (a) Washing clothes   (b) Bathing
    (c) Cleaning utensils   (d) Drying wet clothes

Ans. *(d)* Drying wet clothes is an activity which does not involve use of water.

Q. 2 In which of the following activities will you use minimum amount of water?

    (a) Bathing   (b) Brushing teeth   (c) Washing clothes (d) Mopping a room

Ans. *(b)* In brushing teeth we use minimum amount of water.

Q. 3 The quantity of water required to produce one page of your book is

    (a) one bucket   (b) ten buckets   (c) two glasses   (d) few drops

Ans. *(c)* Two glasses of water is required to produce one page of our book.

Q. 4 Water in our tap comes from a

    (a) river   (b) lake   (c) well   (d) All of these

Ans. *(d)* Water in our tap comes from river, lake or well.

Q. 5 In which of the following cases, evaporation of water will be slowest?

    (a) A tray of water kept in sunlight   (b) A kettle of water kept on a burner
    (c) A glass of water kept in a room   (d) A bucket of water kept on rooftop

Ans. *(c)* The rate of evaporation increases on increasing the temperature and on increasing the surface area. A glass of water kept in a room has minimum surface area in the given options, so rate of evaporation will be slowest.

Q. 6 Transpiration is a process in which plants

    (a) receive water from soil   (b) absorb water vapour from air
    (c) prepare food from water   (d) release water in the form of water vapour

Ans. *(d)* Transpiration is a process in which there is loss of water from plants as water vapour through the pores of their leaves.

Q. 7 Clouds are
- (a) tiny drops of water floating in air
- (b) mixture of dust and water vapour
- (c) particles of water vapour
- (d) rain drops in air

Ans. *(a)* The mass of tiny droplets formed by the condensation of water vapour which we see floating high in the atmosphere is called a cloud.

Q. 8 Wells are fed by
- (a) pond water
- (b) lake water
- (c) rainwater
- (d) groundwater

Ans. *(d)* Wells are fed by groundwater. The underground water can be taken out by digging a well into the ground. It is called well water.

Q. 9 Floods cause extensive damage to
- (a) crops
- (b) property and human life
- (c) domestic animals
- (d) All of these

Ans. *(d)* Floods cause extensive damage to crop fields, villages and forests causing damage to property, human life, domestic animals, crops and wild animals of the forests.

Q. 10 'Catch water where it falls' is the basic idea behind
- (a) recycling of water
- (b) making dams to store water
- (c) rainwater harvesting
- (d) condensation of water vapour

Ans. *(c)* 'Catch water where it falls' is the basic idea behind rainwater harvesting.

Very Short Answer Type Questions

Q. 11 Look at the figure

Write down the activities shown in this figure in which water is being used.

Ans. Activities shown in the above figure are :
- (i) Washing clothes
- (ii) Bathing

Q. 12 Write any two activities which require more than a bucket of water.

Ans. Two activities which require use of more than one bucket of water is washing more than 10 clothes and irrigating a crop field.

Q. 13 Write any two activities which require less than one bucket of water.

Ans. Two activities which require use of less than one bucket of water is brushing teeth and washing a handkerchief.

Short Answer Type Questions

Q. 14 Why do wet clothes placed on a clothes line dry after sometime? Explain.

Ans. Wet clothes placed on a clothes line dry after sometime because water present in wet clothes is converted into water vapour and released in atmosphere due to evaporation which leaves them dry.

Q. 15 Water kept in sunlight gets heat from the sun and is evaporated. But how does water kept under the shade of a tree also gets evaporated? Explain.

Ans. Water kept under the shade of a tree also evaporates because of warm air. Actually, during day time, the heat given out by the sun heats all the air around us. This warm air provides heat for evaporation of water kept in the shade.

Q. 16 How do the areas covered with concrete affect the availability of groundwater?

Ans. Areas covered with concrete affect the availability of groundwater because concrete reduces the seepage of rainwater into the ground which leads to reduction in the availability of groundwater.

Q. 17 Why is there a need for conserving water? Give two reasons.

Ans. There is a need for conserving water because of the following reasons:

(i) Increasing population is creating more demand for usable water.

(ii) Availability of freshwater is decreasing day-by-day.

Q. 18 Water, as ...... goes into atmosphere by the processes of ...... and ...... and forms ......, which on condensation fall in the form of ...... and .... .

Ans. vapours, evaporation, transpiration, clouds, rains, snow/hails

Long Answer Type Questions

Q. 19 Most of the water that falls on the land as rain and snow, sooner or later goes back to a sea or an ocean. Explain how it happens.

Ans. The process by which land water returns back to a sea or an ocean is as follows:

(i) Snow/Rain falling on the mountains melts into water that flows down in the form of streams and rivers.

(ii) A part of the rainwater gets absorbed into the ground and rest flow in the form of stream or rivers.

(iii) The river water after passing through various regions ultimately reaches into a sea or an ocean.

Q. 20 Draw a diagram to show how sea water reaches a lake or pond?

Ans. Sea water reaches a lake or pond is represented by a diagram:

Q. 21 Dissolve two spoons of common salt in half a cup of water. Now, if you want to get the salt back, what will you do?

Ans. The common salt dissolved in half a cup of water can be recovered by removing the water from the salt solution.

This can be done by heating the solution on a gas stove or keeping it under the sun in a plate for few hours.

Due to evaporation of water in both the processes, we will get the salt back.

Q. 22 Explain the process of rooftop rainwater harvesting with the help of a suitable diagram.

Ans. The process of rooftop rainwater harvesting is as follows :

(i) In this process, the rainwater is collected on the rooftop.

(ii) This collected rainwater in allowed to pass through pipes into a storage tank at the ground level.

(iii) The collected water is filtered and used when required.

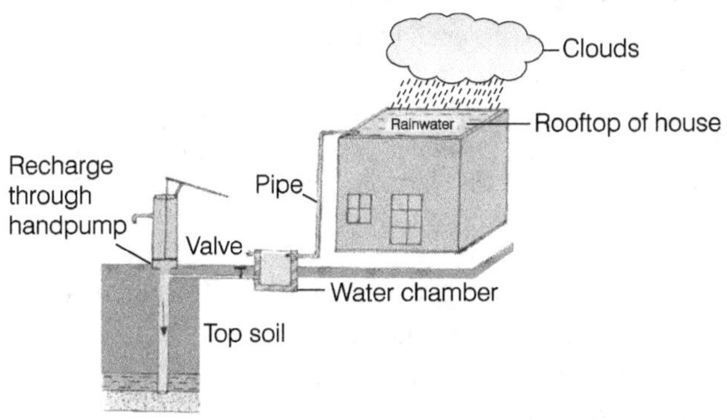

Rooftop rainwater harvesting system

15

Air Around Us

Multiple Choice Questions (MCQs)

Q. 1 Which of the following statements is incorrect?
- (a) All living things require air to breathe
- (b) We can feel air but we cannot see it
- (c) Moving air makes it possible to fly a kite
- (d) Air is present everywhere but not in soil

Ans. *(d)* Air is present everywhere even in the soil. Oxygen is trapped in the soil and is helpful for organisms present in the soil for breathing.

> **Note** *The animals which live in soil and the plant roots which grow in soil need oxygen to breathe.*

Q. 2 Wind does not help in the movement of which of the following?
- (a) Firki
- (b) Weather cock
- (c) Ceiling fan
- (d) Sailing yacht

Ans. *(c)* Wind does not help in movement of ceiling fan. It rotates by electricity.

Q. 3 What is not true about air?
- (a) It makes the windmill rotate
- (b) It helps in the movement of aeroplanes
- (c) Birds can fly due to presence of air
- (d) It has no role in water cycle

Ans. *(d)* The presence of water vapour in air is important for the working of water cycle in nature (This is because it is water vapour present in air which rises high in the sky along with hot air, gets cooled, condenses to form clouds and then brings rain on the earth).

Q. 4 Mountaineers carry oxygen cylinders with them because
- (a) there is no oxygen on high mountains
- (b) there is deficiency of oxygen on mountains at higher altitude
- (c) oxygen is used for cooking
- (d) oxygen keeps them warm at low temperature

Ans. *(b)* As we go up above the sea level, the atmospheric pressure goes on decreasing and the amount of oxygen also decreases at higher altitude. This is why, mountaineers carry oxygen, cylinders with them.

Q. 5 Boojho took an empty plastic bottle, turned it upside down and dipped its open mouth into a bucket filled with water. He then tilted the bottle slightly and made the following observations:

(i) Bubbles of air came out from the bottle.

(ii) Some water entered into the bottle.

(iii) Nitrogen gas came out in the form of bubbles and oxygen gas dissolved in water.

(iv) No bubbles formed, only water entered into the bottle.

Which observation(s) is/are correct?

(a) (i) and (ii)   (b) Only (iv)

(c) (iii) and (iv)   (d) Only (i)

Ans. *(a)* Bubbles of air came out from the bottle and some water entered into the bottle, when it was tilted.

Q. 6 Which of the following components of air is present in the largest amount in the atmosphere?

(a) Nitrogen   (b) Oxygen

(c) Water vapour   (d) Carbon dioxide

Ans. *(a)* Nitrogen is present in the largest amount in the atmosphere. It occupies 78.09% of atmosphere.

Q. 7 The components of air which are harmful to living beings are

(a) nitrogen and carbon dioxide

(b) dust and water vapour

(c) dust and smoke

(d) smoke and water vapour

Ans. *(c)* Dust and smoke present in air are harmful to living beings.

> **Note** *Breathing in air containing smoke and dust may enter our respiratory system (lungs, etc.) and damage our health.*

Q. 8 Usha took a lump of dry soil in a glass and added water to it till it was completely immersed. She observed bubbles coming out. The bubbles contain

(a) water vapour

(b) only oxygen gas

(c) air

(d) None of the above

Ans. *(c)* The bubbles contain air because soil absorbs some amount of air. The air is present in the spaces between the soil particles.

Very Short Answer Type Questions

Q. 9 State whether the following statements are true or false. If false, correct them.

(a) Plants consume oxygen for respiration.

(b) Plants produce oxygen during the process of making their own food.

(c) Air helps in the movements of sailing yachts and glider but plays no role in the flight of birds and aeroplanes.

(d) Air does not occupy any space.

Ans. (a) True   (b) True

(c) False, air also helps in the flight of birds and aeroplanes.

(d) False, air occupies space, i.e. Air fills all the space available to it.

Q. 10 In a number of musical instruments, air plays an important role. Can you name some such instruments?

Ans. Air plays an important role in number of musical instruments such as flute, trumpet, harmonium, shahnai.

Q. 11 In the boxes of Column I, the letters of some words got jumbled. Arrange them in proper form in the boxes given in Column II.

	Column I		Column II
(a)	D I L L M W I N	(a)	
(b)	Y N O G X E	(b)	
(c)	M E S K O	(c)	
(d)	T U D S	(d)	

Ans. (a) Windmill   (b) Oxygen

(c) Smoke   (d) Dust

Q. 12 Make sentences using the given set of words.

(a) 99%, oxygen, nitrogen, air, together

(b) Respiration, dissolved, animals, air, aquatic

(c) Air, wind, motion, called

Ans. The correct sentences are :

(a) Oxygen and nitrogen together make up 99% of the air.

(b) Aquatic animals use dissolved air for respiration.

(c) Air in motion is called wind.

Short Answer Type Questions

Q. 13 A list of words is given in a box. Use appropriate words to fill up the blanks in the following statements.

Air, oxygen, wind, water, vapour, mixture, combination, direction, road, bottles, cylinders.

(a) The ...... makes the windmill rotate.

(b) Air is a ...... of some gases.

(c) A weather cock shows the ...... in which the air is moving at that place.

(d) Mountaineers carry oxygen ...... with them, while climbing high mountains.

Ans. (a) wind   (b) mixture

      (c) direction   (d) cylinders

Q. 14 Observe the given figure carefully and answer the following questions:

(a) What is covering the nose and mouth of the policeman?

(b) Why is he putting a cover on his nose?

(c) Can you comment on air quality of the place as shown in the figure?

Ans. (a) Mask is covering the nose and mouth of the policeman.

    (b) Policeman is putting a cover on his nose to save himself from dirt/polluted air.

    (c) Air quality of the place is not good. It is due to the smoke and gases emitted by the automobiles along with dust particles present in the air.

Q. 15 Garima observed that when she left her tightly capped bottle full of water in the open sunlight, tiny bubbles were formed all around inside the bottle. Help Garima to know why it so happened?

Ans. Air is dissolved in water in the form of oxygen. When water bottle is left in the open sunlight, tiny bubbles were formed all around inside the bottle because air dissolved in water starts escaping in the form of tiny bubbles due to heat from the sun.

Q. 16 Match the Column I with Column II.

	Column I		Column II
(a)	Weather cock	(i)	Gases and fine dust particles
(b)	Mountaineers	(ii)	Sailing yacht
(c)	Fine hair inside the nose	(iii)	Oxygen cylinders
(d)	Smoke	(iv)	Direction of air flow
(e)	Wind	(v)	Prevent dust particles

Ans. The correct matching is as given:

(a)—(iv), (b)—(iii), (c)—(v), (d)—(i), (e)—(ii)

Long Answer Type Questions

Q. 17 Explain the following observations briefly.

(a) A firki does not rotate in a closed area.

(b) The arrow of weather cock points towards a particular direction at a particular moment.

(c) An empty glass in fact is not empty.

(d) Breathing through mouth may harm you.

Ans. (a) Motion of firki is based on the pressure/force applied by air on the blades of the firki. A firki does not rotate in a closed area because of lack of air movement.

(b) The arrow of weather cock points towards a particular direction as it shows the direction in which the air is moving at that place at a particular moment.

(c) An empty glass in fact is not empty. It is filled with air. Air is present everywhere.

(d) Breathing through mouth may harm us because we may inhale dust if present in air which may enter our respiratory system (lungs, etc.) and damage out health.

Q. 18 Write a few sentences for an imaginary situation if any of the following gases disappear from the atmosphere.

(a) Oxygen

(b) Nitrogen

(c) Carbon dioxide

Ans. (a) There will be no life on the earth. Oxygen is vital for life. It helps in burning, respiration, photosynthesis, etc. Oxygen is basic need of all living beings.

(b) Nitrogen does not support burning. If nitrogen gas disappear from the atmosphere, things will burn very fast.

(c) Carbon dioxide is needed for photosynthesis which occurs in green plants. In its absence, plants will not be able to prepare their food and hence, without carbon dioxide there would be no plants or animals on the earth.

Q. 19 Paheli kept some water in a beaker for heating. She observed that tiny bubbles appeared before the water started to boil. She boiled the water for about 5 min and filled it in a bottle upto the brim and kept the bottle airtight till cooled down to room temperature.

(a) Why did the tiny bubbles appeared?

(b) Do you think tiny bubbles will appear on heating the water taken out from the bottle? Justify your answer.

Ans. (a) Air is dissolved in water in the form of oxygen. Tiny bubbles are formed, when air present in the water escape on boiling it.

So, tiny bubbles appeared due to the evolution of air dissolved in water.

(b) No, tiny bubbles will not appear as there is no dissolved air in this water.

Q. 20 On a Sunday morning, Paheli's friend visited her home. She wanted to see some flowering plants in the nearby garden. Both of them went to the garden. While returning from the garden, they also observed some flowering plants on the roadside. But to their surprise, they found that the leaves and flowers of these roadside plants were comparatively very dull. Can you help them to know why?

Ans. The leaves and flowers of the roadside plants are very dull because the air along the roadside is polluted with air pollutants due to emissions from vehicles and industries, etc.

Thus, the roadside plants had probably some dust and soot deposited on them. This made them to appear dull.

16

Garbage In, Garbage Out

Multiple Choice Questions (MCQs)

Q. 1 The method of preparing compost with the help of earthworms, is called

    (a) composting   (b) vermicomposting

    (c) manuring   (d) decomposing

Ans. *(b)* Vermicomposting is a method of preparing compost with the help of earthworms. It is an excellent method of getting the best out of waste and also save a lot of money that is spent on buying expensive chemical fertilisers and manure from the market.

Q. 2 If you dump kitchen waste in a pit, it may, after sometime

    (a) convert into compost

    (b) convert into vermicompost

    (c) remain as such

    (d) remain forever in its dried form

Ans. *(a)* The kitchen waste dumped in a pit may convert into compost after sometime. Kitchen waste is biodegradable and can be decomposed by microorganisms into compost, which is used as a manure. Compost is a natural fertiliser.

Q. 3 Which of the following activities does not reflect responsible behaviour with regard to waste disposal?

    (a) Goods carried in paper bags or cloth bags

    (b) Waste collected in polythene bags for disposal

    (c) Waste separated into those that degrade and those that do not

    (d) Making handicrafts with used up notebooks

Ans. *(b)* Waste collected in polythene bags for disposal does not reflect responsible behaviour. This is because polythene bags are non-biodegradable. They do not decompose in nature on their own and are eaten up along with garbage food by cattle, thus causing harm to them.

Q. 4 Paheli gave the following ill effects of the practice of burning dried leaves and other plant parts

  (a) Burning degrades the soil.
  (b) Burning produces harmful gases/fumes.
  (c) Precious raw materials to obtain manure at low cost is lost.
  (d) Lost of heat is generated unnecessarily.

The correct reasons of why we should not burn leaves are

(a) i, ii and iv   (b) i, ii, iii and iv
(c) ii and iii   (d) ii, iii, and iv

Ans. *(b)* The practice of burning dried leaves and other plant parts leads to all the ill affects mentioned above.
The best way to deal with this waste is to convert it into useful compost.

Q. 5 A garbage collector separate items mentioned below in the garbage into red, green and blue containers for their transfer to landfill, composting pit and recycling unit, respectively.

  (i) Plastic bags   (ii) Newspaper and journals
  (iii) Screw and nuts   (iv) Vegetable peels
  (v) Metal chips   (vi) Egg shells

Which item were transferred to which bin ?

	RED	GREEN	BLUE
A.	(i) and (iv)	(ii) and (iii)	(v) and (vi)
B.	(i) and (iii)	(ii) and (v)	(iv) and (vi)
C.	(i), (iii) and (v)	(iv) and (vi)	(ii) only
D.	(i) and (v)	(ii) and (iv)	(iii) only

Ans. *(c)* The hazardous waste is dumped in red bin, i.e. plastic bags, screws and nuts and metal chips.
The organic waste is put in green bin, i.e. vegetable peels and egg shells. The recyclable material waste is thrown in blue bin, i.e. newspaper and journals.

Q. 6 The steps required for conversion of kitchen garbage into manure are given below in a jumbled form.

  (i) Put garbage in a pit.
  (ii) Cover the bottom of the pit with sand.
  (iii) Cover the pit loosely with a gunny bag or grass.
  (iv) Add worms.

Which of the following shows the correct sequence of the above steps?

(a) (ii), (i), (iv), (iii)   (b) (i), (ii), (iii), (iv)
(c) (ii), (iv), (i), (iii)   (d) (iv), (i), (ii), (iii)

Ans. *(a)* The correct sequence of the steps are ii → i → iv → iii.
This method of making manure from kitchen garbage using worms is called vermicomposting.

Very Short Answer Type Questions

Q. 7 Read the items mentioned in Columns I and II and fill in the related process in the Column III.

	Column I	Column II	Column III
(a)	Organic waste	Earthworms	(i) ....
(b)	Garbage	Dig pit and fill with garbage	(ii) ....
(c)	Old newspaper	Paper bags	(iii) .....

Ans.   (i) Vermicomposting

(ii) Garbage disposal/landfill

(iii) Recycling

Q. 8 Correct the definitions of certain terms given below by changing only one word.

(a) **Compost** Substances converted into manure for use in industries.

(b) **Landfill** Garbage buried under water in an area.

(c) **Recycling** Reuse of unused material in the same or another form.

Ans.   (a) **Compost** Substance is converted into manure for use in **agricultural fields**.

(b) **Landfill** Garbage is buried under **soil** in an area.

(c) **Recycling** Reuse of **used** material in the same or another form.

Q. 9 Provide the suitable term that expresses the meaning of each of the following statements.

(a) Greeting cards made from newspaper.

(b) Contents of the waste bins.

(c) Worms converting certain kinds of waste into manure.

(d) An area where a lot of garbage is collected, spread out and covered with soil.

Ans.   A suitable term describing/expressing the meaning of the above given statements are as follows:

(a) Recycling

(b) Garbage

(c) Vermicomposting

(d) Landfill

Short Answer Type Questions

Q. 10 To what use can you put the following kinds of garbage and how?

(a) Rotting smelly garbage

(b) Dry leaves collected in a garbage

(c) Old newspapers

Ans. (a) Rotting smelly garbage can be converted into **compost** through composting. The process of converting plant and animal waste materials into manure by rotting is called composting.

(b) Dry leaves collected in a garbage can be used as **manure** by vermicomposting the method of making compost from dry leaves by using red worms is called vermicomposting.

(c) Old newspapers can be **recycled** to make paper bags or paper pulp for handicrafts. Recycling is the process of changing waste material into new products to reduce waste and pollution.

Q. 11 Paheli was writing a letter to her friend. She crumpled and threw the first draft of her letter on the floor as it had become untidy. Similarly, she crumpled and threw 6 more papers on the ground. In the end, she picked them up and put them in a polythene bag and threw it on the road outside her house.

Do you think, Paheli's action were responsible? What would you have done if you were in her place?

Ans. No, in my opinion, Paheli's action were not responsible. She wasted paper and used a polythene bag. If I would have been in her place, I would have used the reverse side of the paper for doing rough work or convert it into paper pulp to make a handicraft item.

Q. 12 Read the poem written below and then answer the questions from the information gathered from the book or elsewhere.

Blue and Green

Two bins, you mean?

Yes, they are there

to throw your waste

But not in a hurry

Nor in a haste.

Select from waste, sieve if seems muddy
Separate all items and when they are ready
Place in a blue bin, or one that is green
For a voyage to the landfill, or for composting.

(a) Name the two kinds of waste that need to be separated from each other in two different waste bins.

(b) Name two items of waste each that need to be sent to a (i) landfill (ii) for composting.

Ans. (a) Two kinds of waste that need to be separated are **biodegradable and non-biodegradable** wastes. The former is part of garbage on which bacteria can act to form harmless substances and the latter is part of garbage that cannot rot or decay.

(b) (i) The part of garbage which cannot be disposed off by other method is dumped in a landfill, e.g. Any metal items.

(ii) The rotted plant and animal waste can be sent for composting. The microorganisms can act on these wastes to convert it into manure.

Q. 13 Beera, a farmer would clear his field everyday and burn dry leaves fallen on the ground. After sometime, he found that those people living in huts near his field were suffering from cough and breathing problems.

    (a) Can you explain, why?

    (b) Also suggest an environment friendly way to dispose the dry leaves.

Ans. (a) Fumes and gases produced by burning dry leaves caused cough and breathing problems for the people living in the nearby area.

    (b) An environment friendly way to dispose the dry leaves is to use them for making manure.

Long Answer Type Questions

Q. 14 Put a tick (✓) against the garbage items given in table which could be converted into manure. Put a cross (✗) against the others.

	Garbage items	Make manure or not		Garbage items	Make manure or not
(i)	Egg shells		(vi)	Nails and screws	
(ii)	Straw		(vii)	Plastic bangles	
(iii)	Dry flowers		(viii)	Left over food	
(iv)	Pebbles		(ix)	Steel broken vessel	
(v)	Broken pieces of glass		(x)	Dead animals	

Ans. The given table shows garbage items that can be converted into manure or not.

	Garbage items	Make manure or not
(i)	Egg shells	✓
(ii)	Straw	✓
(iii)	Dry flowers	✓
(iv)	Pebbles	✗
(v)	Broken pieces of glass	✗
(vi)	Nails and screws	✗
(vii)	Plastic bangles	✗
(viii)	Left over food	✓
(ix)	Steel broken vessel	✗
(x)	Dead animals	✓

Note *The biodegradable waste such as plant and animal waste can be converted into manure.*

Q. 15 The pie charts *A* and *B* shown in the figure are based on waste seggregation method adopted by two families *X* and *Y*, respectively.

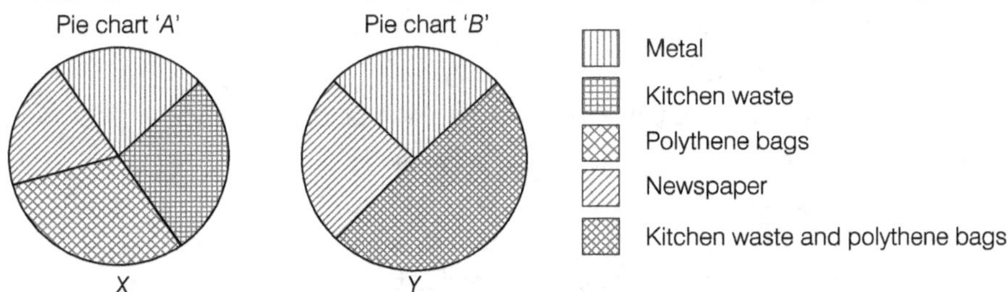

Which of the two families *X* or *Y*, do you think is more environmentally conscious and why?

Ans. The family *X* is more environmentally conscious because they dispose off their kitchen waste and polythene bags separately.

Disposing them separately has an advantage as kitchen waste is biodegradable and can be converted into compost. Polythene bags on the contrary are non-biodegradable and cannot be recycled or decomposed.

Q. 16 Given below are steps in vermicomposting and each step has been given an alphabet. Rearrange the steps in the correct sequence and write the alphabets on the chart provided. One step is done for you.

F Dig a pit in a suitable place in your garden.

C Spread sand on the floor of the pit.

E Add vegetable peels and fruits waste in the pit.

A Sprinkle water to keep it moist.

D Place red worms in the pit.

B Cover with a gunny bag or grass.

Step	1	-	F
	2	-	
	3	-	
	4	-	
	5	-	
	6	-	

Ans. Vermicomposting is a method of composting where compost is made from biodegradable waste with the help of red worms.

The steps in this process are

1	=	F
2	=	C
3	=	E
4	=	B
5	=	A
6	=	D

Q. 17 Write three sentences on what comes to your mind when you get a chance to see the following:

   (a) A rag picker

   (b) A cow eating a polythene bag.

   (c) Foul odour emanating from garbage at the entrance of your house.

Ans.   Following things come to our mind when we see:

   (a) **A rag picker**

   (i) Poor people working due to poverty.

   (ii) He removes the garbage generated by others.

   (iii) He is exposing himself to harmful substances, generated due to toxic waste.

   (b) **A cow eating a polythene bag**

   (i) Cow is getting exposed to hazardous materials, due to our mistake of using polythene bags.

   (ii) There may be a possibility of polythene choking the animal to death.

   (iii) Incorrect/Improper disposal of polythenes by us.

   (c) **Foul odour emanating from garbage at the entrance of our house**

   (i) There must be a large quantity of waste generated in the house.

   (ii) The waste has made the surroundings unhealthy.

   (iii) Unpleasant sight, the waste is disturbing the beauty of the house.

Q. 18 Beautiful handcrafted articles like boxes and toys are made up of paper pulp in our country. Can you explain how paper pulp which is made from paper can be used to make hard boxes and other articles?

Ans.   By following these simple steps, we can make hard boxes or other articles from the recycled paper pulp:

   Step I Create a stencil by unfolding a small, one piece cardboard box and trace it on a piece of cardboard that is the same size as your mold. Then, cut out that shape with scissors.

   Step II Place the box stencil between your mold and deckle.

   Step III Raise the mold, deckle and stencil to the surface in one continuous motion and then remove them from the pulp.

   Step IV Remove the box from the stencil and let the paper dry.

   Step V Assemble the box by folding and gluing or taping the edges. Decorate it as your need.

Q. 19 Recently, a ban on plastic bags has been imposed in many places. Is the ban justified? Give reasons in three sentences.

Ans.   The recent ban on plastic bags is justified because:

   (i) The resources used to create the bags are scarce:

   (ii) They harm the environment when disposed off improperly and also are visible blight of roadside litter.

   (iii) Cost of disposing or recycling them is high, as they are non-biodegradable.

Q. 20 Why should we not burn plastic items?

Ans. We should not burn plastic items because

(i) they do not burn easily.

(ii) they produce toxic gases when burnt and left over ashes are also toxic.

(iii) they add to soil pollution.

(iv) burnt pieces may be eaten by cows which may choke them to death.

(v) toxic gases lead to many respiratory diseases.

Q. 21 What happens when

(a) cooking medium is made to flow down a drain?

(b) insecticides, motor oil, paints are poured down the drain?

(c) tea leaves, cotton swabs and old soft toys are thrown into the drain?

Ans. (a) If cooking medium is made to flow down a drain, it may clog pores in soil and can block pipes also.

(b) If insecticides, motor oil, paints are poured down the drain, this may kill useful microbes which help to purify water.

(c) If tea leaves, cotton swabs and old soft toys are thrown into the drain, it can choke the drains and block the water supply of the area.

Q. 22 Answer the following questions in one or two words or sentences.

(a) Why should we prefer to use paper bags rather than polythene bags?

(b) Who out of the following, should properly dispose of the garbage-father, mother, elder brother, younger sister?

(c) Which one out of beetles, roundworm and earthworm are used for vermicomposting and why?

Ans. (a) We should prefer using paper bags rather than polythene bags as paper can be decomposed of easily. This reduce the generation of plastic garbage.

(b) Every member of the society or family is responsible to dispose of the garbage properly.

(c) Earthworms are the best organisms to be used for vermicomposting as they convert the waste from plants, animals or their products into compost.

www.ingramcontent.com/pod-product-compliance
Lightning Source LLC
LaVergne TN
LVHW020033160726
843469LV00044B/1758